The Tribune of

A Chronicle of Jo

W. L. Grant

Alpha Editions

This edition published in 2024

ISBN : 9789362098818

Design and Setting By
Alpha Editions
www.alphaedis.com
Email - info@alphaedis.com

As per information held with us this book is in Public Domain.
This book is a reproduction of an important historical work. Alpha Editions uses the best technology to reproduce historical work in the same manner it was first published to preserve its original nature. Any marks or number seen are left intentionally to preserve its true form.

Contents

PREFACE .... - 1 -
CHAPTER I NOVA SCOTIA .... - 2 -
CHAPTER II BIRTH AND TRAINING .... - 7 -
CHAPTER III THE OLD COLONIAL SYSTEM ... - 15 -
CHAPTER IV THE FIGHT FOR RESPONSIBLE GOVERNMENT .... - 23 -
CHAPTER V RAILWAYS AND IMPERIAL CONSOLIDATION .... - 42 -
CHAPTER VI BAFFLED HOPES .... - 55 -
BIBLIOGRAPHICAL NOTE .... - 72 -

PREFACE

In May-August 1875 my father, the Rev. G. M. Grant, published in the *Canadian Monthly* four articles on Joseph Howe, which give, in my opinion, the best account ever likely to be written of Howe's character, motives, and influence. Twenty-five years later he had begun to write for the 'Makers of Canada' a life of Howe, but his death left this task to Mr Justice Longley. In this he had thought to incorporate much of his earlier articles, and his copies of them remain in my hands, with excisions and emendations in his own handwriting. In the present little book I have not scrupled to embody these portions of my father's work.

Howe's speeches and public letters are the basis for any story of his career. They were originally published in two volumes in Boston in 1858, nominally edited by William Annand, really by Howe himself. In 1909 a revised edition, with chapters covering the last fourteen years of his life, was published at Halifax, excellently edited by Mr J. A. Chisholm, K.C. The Journals of the Legislative Council and Legislative Assembly of Nova Scotia contain the dispatches from the Colonial Office quoted in the text. Incidents and anecdotes have been taken from the biographies by Mr Joseph Fenety and Mr Justice Longley. I have also consulted the collection of his father's papers presented to the Canadian Archives by Mr Sydenham Howe, and a manuscript life of Howe by his old friend the late George Johnson. Lord Grey, with his invariable interest in things Canadian, has had the private correspondence of his uncle searched for anything that might throw light on the railway imbroglio of 1851, but without result.

W. L. GRANT.

QUEEN'S UNIVERSITY,
KINGSTON, 1914.

CHAPTER I
NOVA SCOTIA

Joseph Howe was in a very special sense at once the child and the father of Nova Scotia. His love for his native province was deep and passionate. He was one in whom her defects and excellences could be seen in bold outline; one who knew and loved her with unswerving love; who caught the inspiration of her woods, streams, and shores; and who gave it back in verses not unmeet, in a thousand stirring appeals to her people, and in that which is always more heroic than words, namely, civic action and life-service. 'Joe' Howe was Nova Scotia incarnate. Once, at a banquet somewhere in England, in responding to the toast of the colonies, he painted the little province he represented with such tints that the chairman at the close announced, in half fun, half earnest, that he intended to pack up his portmanteau that night and start for Nova Scotia, and he advised all present to do the same. 'You boast of the fertility and beauty of England,' said Howe, in a tone of calm superiority; 'why, there's one valley in Nova Scotia where you can ride for fifty miles under apple blossoms.' And, again: 'Talk of the value of land, I know an acre of rocks near Halifax worth more than an acre in London. Scores of hardy fishermen catch their breakfasts there in five minutes, all the year round, and no tillage is needed to make the production continue equally good for a thousand years to come.' In a speech at Southampton his description of her climate was a terse, off-hand statement of facts, true, doubtless, but scarcely the whole truth. 'I rarely wear an overcoat,' said he, 'except when it rains; an old chief justice died recently in Nova Scotia at one hundred and three years of age, who never wore one in his life. Sick regiments invalided to our garrison recover their health and vigour immediately, and yellow fever patients coming home from the West Indies walk about in a few days.' 'Boys,' he said on one occasion to a Nova Scotia audience, 'brag of your country. When I'm abroad I brag of everything that Nova Scotia is, has, or can produce; and when they beat me at everything else, I turn round on them and say, "How high does your tide rise?"' He always had them there—no other country could match the tides of the Bay of Fundy. He loved and he sang of her streams and her valleys, her woods and her wild-flowers, most of all of the 'Mayflower,' the trailing arbutus of early spring, with its fresh pink petals and its wonderful fragrance, long since adopted as the provincial emblem. After more than one political fight he retired to the country for a month or for a year, and there let nature breathe into his soul her beauty and her calm. Of one such occasion he wrote: 'For a month I did nothing but play with the children and read old books to my girls. I then went into the woods and called moose with the old hunters, camping out night after night, listening to their stories, calming my thoughts with the perfect stillness of the forest, and forgetting the bitterness of conflict amid the beauties of nature.'

But while he was thus the child of Nova Scotia, he was her creator as well. Early Nova Scotia was rather a collection of scattered little settlements than a province. To Howe, in great measure, she owed her unity.

The first settlements in the Acadian peninsula were made by the French, in the fertile diked lands at the head of the Bay of Fundy. To the number of six thousand these Acadians were driven out on the eve of the Seven Years' War, a tragedy told of in Longfellow's *Evangeline*. In after years many of them crept back to different parts of their beloved province, and little settlements here and there, from Pubnico in the south to Cheticamp in the north-west, still speak the speech of Old France.

In 1713 the province became British, and in 1749 Halifax was founded by the British government. From this time on, bands of emigrants from various countries settled in districts often widely separated, and established rude farming and fishing communities, very largely self-contained. Howe knew and loved them all. In one of his speeches he thus sketched the process: 'A small band of English adventurers, under Cornwallis, laid the foundation of Halifax. These, at a critical moment, were reinforced by the Loyalist emigration, which flowed into our western counties and laid broad and deep the foundation of their prosperity. A few hardy emigrants from the old colonies and their descendants built up the maritime county of Yarmouth. Two men of that stock first discovered the value of Locke's Island, the commercial centre of East Shelburne. A few hundreds of sturdy Germans peopled the beautiful county of Lunenburg. A handful of emigrants from Yorkshire gave animation to the county of Cumberland. The vale of Colchester has been made to blossom as the rose by the industry of a few adventurers from the north of Ireland. Half a century ago a few poor but pious Lowland Scotsmen penetrated into Pictou. They were followed by a few hundreds of Highlanders, many of them "evicted" from the Duchess of Sutherland's estates. Look at Pictou now, with its beautiful river slopes and fertile mountain settlements, its one hundred schools, its numerous churches and decent congregations, its productive mines and thirty thousand inhabitants, living in comfort and abundance. The picture rises like magic before the eye, and yet every cheerful tint and feature has been supplied by emigration. At the last election it was said that two hundred and seventy Frasers voted in that county—all of them heads of families and proprietors of land. I doubt if as many of the same name can be found in all Scotland who own real estate.'[1]

Thus the little settlements gradually expanded into prosperous fishing and farming communities, on the statistics of whose steadily growing exports and imports Howe loved to dwell. But they long lacked a common consciousness, and no man did so much to knit them together as Howe. Germans of Lunenburg, New Englanders of Annapolis and Cornwallis, Loyalists of Shelburne, Scottish Presbyterians of Pictou, Scottish Roman Catholics of Antigonish, French of Tracadie and Cheticamp, and Irish of Halifax, all learned from him to be Nova Scotians and to 'brag of their country.' The chief influences making for union were the growth of roads, the growth of political discussion, and the growth of newspapers; and to all three Howe contributed. Both as politician and as editor he toured the province from end to end, walked, drove, or rode along the country lanes, and in learning to love its every nook and cranny taught its people their duty to one another and to the province. In those days when there were few highways, and bridle-paths were dignified with the name of roads; when the fishermen and farmers along the coast did their business with Halifax by semi-annual visits in their boats or smacks; when the postmen carried Her Majesty's mail to Annapolis in a queer little gig that could accommodate one passenger; when the mail to Pictou and the Gulf of St Lawrence was stowed away in one of the great-coat pockets of a sturdy pedestrian, who kept the other pocket free for the partridges he shot on the way, we can fancy what an event in any part of the province the appearance of Joe Howe must have been.

Halifax, the capital, where Howe was born, engrossed most of the social and political life of the province; in fact, it *was* the province. The only other port in Nova Scotia proper that vessels could enter with foreign produce was Pictou. A few Halifax merchants did all the trade. Halifax was an old city, as colonial cities count. It was near Great Britain as compared with Quebec, Kingston, or Toronto; much nearer, relatively, then than now. The harbour was open all the year round, giving unbroken communication with the mother country. Halifax had a large garrison, and it was the summer headquarters of the North American fleet. On these and other accounts it seemed to be the most desirable place for a British gentleman to settle in, and many accordingly did settle in it. Their children entered the Army or Navy or Civil Service, and many distinguished themselves highly.

Halifax was essentially a naval and military town. As such it was proud of its great traditions. It was into Halifax Harbour, on Whitsunday 1813, just as the bells were calling to church, that the *Shannon* towed the *Chesapeake*. Captain Broke had been wounded and the first lieutenant killed, and the *Shannon* was commanded by a Halifax boy, her second lieutenant. Of these glories no one was prouder than Howe. 'On some of the hardest fought fields of the Peninsula,' he said, 'my countrymen died in the front rank, with their faces to the foe. The proudest naval trophy of the last American war was brought by a Nova Scotian into the harbour of his native town; and the blood that flowed from Nelson's death-wound in the cockpit of the *Victory* mingled with that of a Nova Scotian stripling beside him, struck down in the same glorious fight.'[2]

On summer nights the whole population turned out to hear the regimental band. One of the great functions of the week was the Sunday church parade of the garrison to St Paul's Church, which had been built in the year of the founding of the city. On these occasions the scarlet and ermine of the chief justice vied in splendour with the gold lace of the admiral and of the general. Whether this was altogether good for the town may be doubted. It gave the young men of civilian families a tendency to ape the military classes and to despise business. The private soldiers and non-commissioned officers, with little to do in the piping times of peace, took to the dissipations of the garrison town. Drunkenness was common, though not more so than in the England of that day. 'I ask you,' said Howe in his first great speech, 'if ever you knew a town of the size and respectability of Halifax where the peace was worse preserved? Scarcely a night passes that there are not cries of murder in the upper streets; scarcely a day that there are not two or three fights upon the wharves.'

Yet along with the drink and the snobbishness went much of finer grain. Many of the British officers brought traditions and standards of social life and of culture sometimes lacking in the Canada of to-day. At the dinner-tables of Halifax in the early nineteenth century, when the merchant aristocracy dined the officers, the standard of manners was often high and the range of the conversation wide.

From the rest of British North America Nova Scotia was cut off by hundreds of miles of tumbled, lake-studded rock and hill. Its intercourse with the outer world was wholly by sea. The larger loyalty was to England across the Atlantic. It was by sea that Halifax traded with St John and Boston and Portland, which were a hundred times better known in Nova Scotia than were Montreal and Toronto. The staple trade of the merchants was with the West Indies, to which they sent fish and coal and lumber, receiving in return sugar and rum and molasses. Most of this sea-borne commerce centred at Halifax, rather to the detriment of the rest of the province, for from Halifax inland the ways were rough and difficult. But gradually the other coast towns won their privileges and became ports of entry. At Pictou, especially, the industry of building wooden ships grew up, which, until knocked on the head by the use of iron and steel, made Nova Scotian industry known on every sea, and gave her in the fifties a larger tonnage than all the other British colonies combined.

[1] Chisholm, *Speeches and Letters*, vol. ii, p. 177.

[2] See *The War with the United States*, chap. v.

CHAPTER II
BIRTH AND TRAINING

Howe was born on the 13th of December 1804, in an old-fashioned cottage on the steep hill that rises up from the city side of the Northwest Arm, a beautiful inlet of the sea stealing up from the entrance of the harbour for three or four miles into the land behind the city of Halifax. A 'lawn with oak-trees round the edges,' a little garden and orchard with apple and cherry trees, surrounded the house. Behind, sombre pine-groves shut it out from the world, and in front, at the foot of the hillside, the cheery waters of the 'Arm' ebbed and flowed in beauty. On the other side of the water, which is not much more than a quarter of a mile wide, rose knolls clothed with almost every native variety of wood, and bare rocky hills, with beautiful little bays sweeping round their feet and quiet coves eating in here and there. A vast country, covered with boulders and dotted with lovely lakes, stretched far beyond. Amid these surroundings the boy grew up, and his love of nature grew with him. In later years he was never tired of praising the 'Arm's enchanted ground,' while for the Arm itself his feelings were those of a lover for his mistress. Here is a little picture he recalls to his sister Jane's memory in after days:

Not a cove but still retaineth
Wavelets that we loved of yore,
Lightly up the rock-weeds lifting,
Gently murmuring o'er the sand;
Like romping girls each other chasing,
Ever brilliant, ever shifting,
Interlaced and interlacing,
Till they sink upon the strand.

In his boyish days he haunted these shores, giving to them every hour he could snatch from school or work. He became very fond of the water, and was always much at home in it. He loved the trees and the flowers; but naturally enough, as a healthy boy should, he loved swimming, rowing, skating, lobster-spearing by torch-light, or fishing, much more. He himself describes these years:

The rod, the gun, the spear, the oar,
I plied by lake and sea—
Happy to swim from shore to shore,
Or rove the woodlands free.

In the summer months he went to a school in the city, taught by a Mr Bromley on Lancaster's system. 'What kind of a boy was Joe?' was asked of an old lady who had gone to school with him sixty years before. 'Why, he was a regular dunce; he had a big nose, a big mouth, and a great big ugly head; and he used to chase me to death on my way home from school,' was her ready answer. It is easy to picture the eager, ugly, bright-eyed boy, fonder of a frolic with the girls than of Dilworth's spelling-book. He never had a very handsome face; his features were not chiselled, and the mould was not Grecian. Face and features were Saxon; the eyes light blue, and full of kindly fun. In after years, when he filled and rounded out, he had a manly open look, illumined always as by sunlight for his friends, and a well-proportioned, 'buirdly' form, that well entitled him to the name of man in Queen Elizabeth's full sense of the word. And when his face glowed with the inspiration that burning thoughts and words impart, and his great deep chest swelled and broadened, he looked noble indeed. His old friends describe him as having been a splendid-looking fellow in his best days; while old foes just as honestly assure you that he always had a 'common' look. It is easy to understand that both impressions of him could be justifiably entertained. Very decided merits of expression were needed to compensate for the total absence of beard and for the white face, into which only strong excitement brought any glow of colour.

Howe was fortunate in his father. John Howe was a Loyalist, of Puritan stock which had come to Massachusetts in the seventeenth century. When the American Revolution broke out, alone of his family he was true to the British flag. Many years afterwards his son told a Boston audience that his father 'learned the printing business in this city. He had just completed his apprenticeship, and was engaged to a very pretty girl, when the Revolution broke out. He saw the battle of Bunker's Hill from one of the old houses here; he nursed the wounded when it was over. Adhering to the British side, he was driven out at the evacuation, and retired to Newport, where his betrothed followed him. They were married there, and afterwards settled at Halifax. He left all his household goods and gods behind him, carrying away nothing but his principles and the pretty girl.'

In politics John Howe was a high Tory; in religion a dissenter of the dissenters, belonging to a small sect known as Sandemanians. But neither narrow orthodoxy in politics nor narrow heterodoxy in religion can hide from us the noble, self-less character of Joe Howe's father. No matter how early in the morning his son might get up, if there was any light in the eastern sky, there was the old gentleman sitting at the window, the Bible on his knee. On Sunday mornings he would start early to meet the little flock to whom for many years he preached in an upper room, not as an ordained minister, but as a brother who had gifts—who could expound the Word in a strain of simple eloquence. Puritan in character, in faith, and in devotion to a simple ritual, he gave token that the Puritan organ of combativeness was not undeveloped in him. As a magistrate, also, he doubtless believed that the sword should not be borne in vain; and being an unusually tall, stately man, possessing immense physical strength, he could not have been pleasant in the eyes of law-breakers. The story is told that one Sunday afternoon, as Mr Howe was walking homewards, Bible under his arm, Joe trotting by his side, they came upon two men fighting out their little differences. The old gentleman sternly commanded them to desist, but, very naturally, they only paused long enough to answer him with raillery. 'Hold my Bible, Joe,' said his father. Taking hold of each of the combatants by the neck, and swinging them to and fro as if they were a couple of noisy newspaper boys, he bumped their heads together two or three times; then, with a lunge from the left shoulder, followed by another from the right, he sent them staggering off, till brought up by the ground some twenty or thirty feet apart. 'Now, lads,' calmly remarked the mighty magistrate to the prostrate twain, 'let this be a lesson to you not to break the Sabbath in future'; and, taking his Bible under his arm, he and Joe resumed their walk homewards, the little fellow gazing up with a new admiration on the slightly flushed but always beautiful face of his father. As boy or man, the son never wrote or spoke of him but with reverence. 'For thirty years,' he once said, 'he was my instructor, my play-fellow, almost my daily companion. To him I owe my fondness for reading, my familiarity with the Bible, my knowledge of old Colonial and American incidents and characteristics. He left me nothing but his example and the memory of his many virtues, for all that he ever earned was given to the poor. He was too good for this world; but the remembrance of his high principles, his cheerfulness, his childlike simplicity and truly Christian character, is never absent from my mind.' It was John Howe's practice for years 'to take his Bible under his arm every Sunday afternoon, and, assembling around him in the large room all the prisoners in the Bridewell, to read and explain to them the Word of God.... Many were softened by his advice and won by his example; and I have known him to have them, when their time had expired, sleeping unsuspected beneath his roof, until they could get employment in the country.' So testified his son concerning him in Halifax. When too old to do any regular work, he often visited the houses of the poor and infirm in the city and beyond Dartmouth, filling his pockets at a grocer's with packages of tea and sugar before setting out on his expeditions.

After the Revolution Great Britain was not regardless of her exiled children. She treated the Loyalists with a liberality far exceeding that of the United States to the war-worn soldiers of Washington. John Howe was rewarded with the offices of King's Printer, and Postmaster-General of Nova Scotia,

Cape Breton, Prince Edward Island, New Brunswick, and the Bermudas. But in spite of these high-sounding titles, the family income was small, and all the economies of Joe's mother—his father's second wife, a shrewd practical Nova Scotian widow—could not stretch it very far. At the age of thirteen young Joe was told that he must go to work. His eldest brother had succeeded to his father's positions, and into the printing-office the boy was sent. He began at the lowest rung of the ladder, learned his trade from the bottom upwards, sweeping out the office, delivering the *Gazette*, and doing all the multitudinous errands and jobs of printer's boy before he attained to the dignity of setting up type. 'So you're the devil,' said a judge to him on one occasion when the boy was called on as a witness. 'Yes, sir, in the office, but not in the Court House,' he at once answered, with a look and gesture that threw the name back on his lordship, to the great amusement of all present.

His education went on while he learned his trade. The study of books, talks in the long evenings with his father, and intimate loving communion with nature, all contributed to build up his character. While he read everything he could lay hold of, the Bible and Shakespeare were his great teachers. He knew these thoroughly, and to his intimate acquaintance with them he owed that pure well of English undefiled which streamed with equal readiness from his lips and his pen. His taste was formed on English classics, not on cheap novels. His knowledge, not only of the great highways of English literature, but of its nooks, corners, and byways, was singularly thorough. In after years it could easily be seen in his speeches that his knowledge was not of the kind that is crammed for the occasion. It flowed from him without effort, and gave a charm to his ordinary conversation. Though living in the city during his teens, he spent as much of his time at home as he possibly could. He loved the woods, and as he seldom got away from work on a week day, he often spent Sundays among the trees in preference to attending the terribly long-drawn-out Sandemanian service.

His apprenticeship itself was a process of self-education. He worked the press from morn till night, and found in the dull metal the knowledge and the power he loved. One woman—a relative—taught him French. With other women, who were attracted by his brightness, he read the early English dramatists and the more modern poets, especially Campbell, Mrs Hemans, and Byron. He delighted in fun and frolic and sports of all kinds, and was at the head of everything. But amid all his reading and his companionships elsewhere, he never forgot home. He would go out to it in the evening, as often as he could, and after a long swim in the Arm would spend the night with his father. One evening his love for home saved him from drowning. Running out from town and down to the water below the house, he plunged in as usual, but, when a little distance out from shore, was seized with cramp. The remedies in such a case—to kick vigorously or throw oneself on one's back and float—are just the remedies a man feels utterly unable at the time to try. He was alone and drowning when, his eye being turned at the moment to the cottage upon the hillside, he saw the candle for the night just being placed on the window-sill. The light arrested him, and 'there will be sorrow there to-morrow when I'm missed' passed through his mind. The thought made him give so fierce a kick that he fairly kicked the cramp out of his leg. A few strokes brought him to the shore, where he sank down utterly exhausted with excitement.

Had he been anything of a coward, this experience would have kept him from solitary swims for the rest of his life. But he was too fond of the water to give it up so easily. When working in after years at his own paper, midnight often found him at the desk or at the press. After such toil most young men would have gone upstairs (for he lived above his office then) and thrown themselves on their beds, all tired and soiled with ink; but for six or seven months in the year his practice was to throw off his apron and run down to the market slip, and soon the moon or the stars saw him bobbing like a wild duck in the harbour. Cleaned, braced in nerve, and all aglow, he would run back again, and be sleeping the sleep of the just ten minutes after. When tired with literary or political work, a game of rackets always revived him. There was not a better player in Halifax, civilian or military. To his latest days he urged boys to practise manly sports and exercises of all kinds.

Such a boy, fond of communing with nature, with young blood running riot in his veins, and with wild vague ideals and passions intertwined in his heart, inevitably took to writing poetry. But though he had the poet's heart, he had not the concentration of the great poet. All through his life he loved to string together verses, grave and gay. Some of his pasquinades are very clever; some of his serious verse is mellifluous enough; but as a poet he is not even a minor bard. Yet one of his early effusions, named *Melville Island*, written when he was twenty, was not without influence on his future. Such was its merit that Sir Brenton Halliburton, a very grand old gentleman indeed, went out of his way to compliment the lad and to advise him to cultivate his powers. The few words of praise from a man deservedly respected roused in Howe the high resolve to make letters his career. He deluged the local newspapers with prose and verse, much of which was accepted. In 1827, when just twenty-three years of age, he and another lad bought the *Weekly Chronicle*, and changed its name to the *Acadian*, with Howe as editor-in-chief. Before the year had ended his young ambition urged him to sell out to his partner and to buy a larger and more ambitious paper, the *Nova Scotian*, into possession of which he entered in January 1828. To find the purchase-money he did not hesitate to go deeply into debt.

In the same month he added to his responsibilities and his happiness by his marriage with Catharine Susan Ann Macnab. Men's wives bulk less largely in their biographies than in their lives. Mrs Howe's sweetness and charm were an unfailing strength to her husband. She moderated his extravagance, and bore cheerfully with his habit, so trying to a housekeeper, of filling the house with his friends at all hours and at every meal. Above all, she never nagged, or said 'I told you so.' She believed in him and in his work, and cheered him in his hours of depression. A man of such buoyant feelings, with such charm of manner, was quick to feel the attractions of the bright eyes of the pretty Nova Scotian girls. Many a wife would have taken deep offence at her husband's numerous but superficial flirtations, but Mrs Howe knew better; and when in 1840 he was called out to fight a duel, he could say with truth, in a letter which he wrote to her, and which he entrusted to a friend to be delivered in case he should not return: 'I cannot trust myself to write what I feel. You had my boyish heart, and have shared my love and entire confidence up to this hour.'

Thus in January 1828 Howe found himself with a wife to support and a newspaper to establish. He had to fight with his own hand, and to fight single-handed. When he commenced, he had not 'a single individual, with one exception, capable of writing a paragraph, upon whom he could fall back.' He had to do all himself: to report the debates in the House of Assembly and important trials in the courts, to write the local items as well as the editorials, to prepare digests of British, foreign, and colonial news; in a word, to 'run the whole machine.' He wrote voluminous descriptions of every part of the province that he visited, under the title of 'Eastern and Western Ramblings.' Those rambles laid the foundation of much of his future political power and popularity. He became familiar not only with the province and the character and extent of its resources, but also with every nook and corner of the popular heart. He graduated with honours at the only college he ever attended—what he called 'the best of colleges—a farmer's fireside.' He was admirably qualified physically and socially for this kind of life. He didn't know that he had a digestion, and was ready to eat anything and to sleep anywhere. These were strong points in his favour; for in the hospitable countryside of Nova Scotia, if a visitor does not eat a Benjamin's portion, the good woman of the house suspects that he does not like the food, and that he is pining for the dainties of the city. He would talk farm, fish, or horse with the people as readily as politics or religion. He made himself, or rather he really felt, equally at home in the fisherman's cabin or the log-house of the new settler as with the substantial farmer or well-to-do merchant; he would kiss the women, remember all about the last sickness of the baby, share the jokes of the men and the horse-play of the lads, and be popular with all alike. He came along fresh, hearty, healthy, full of sunlight, brimming over with news, fresh from contact with the great people in Halifax,—yet one of the plain people, hailing them Tom and Jack, and as happy with them as if in the king's palace. 'Joe Howe came to our house last night,' bragged a little girl as she skipped along to school next morning; 'he kissed mamma and kissed me too.' The familiarity was seldom rebuked, for his heartiness was contagious. He was as full of jokes as a pedlar, and had as few airs. A brusqueness of manner and coarseness of speech, which was partly natural, became thus ingrained in him, and party struggles subsequently coarsened his moral fibre. From this absence of refinement flowed a lack of perception of the fitting that often made him speak loosely, even when men and women were by to whom such a style gave positive pain. No doubt much of his coarseness, like that of every humorist, was based on honesty and hatred of shams. When he saw silly peacocks strutting about and trying to fill the horizon with their tails, he could not help ruffling their feathers and making them scream, were it only to let the world know how unmelodious were their voices. It was generally in the presence of prudes that he referred to unnamable things; and he most affected low phrases when he talked to very superfine people. Still, the vein of coarseness was in him, like the baser stuffs in the ores of precious metals; but his literary taste kept his writings pure.

From his twenty-third to his thirty-first year his education went on in connection with his editorial and other professional work. He became intimate with the leading men in the town. He had trusty friends all over the country. His paper and he were identified as paper and editor have seldom been. All correspondence was addressed, not to an unknown figure of vast, ill-defined proportions called Mr Editor, but simply to Joseph Howe. Even when it was known that he was absent in Europe, the country correspondence always came, and was published in the old way:

'Mr Joseph Howe, Sir———.' He cordially welcomed literary talent of all kinds, giving every man full swing on his own hobby, and changing rapidly from grave to gay, from lively to severe. He cultivated from the first the journalistic spirit of giving fair play in his columns to both sides, even when one of the sides was the editor or the proprietor. After he entered the House of Assembly, the speeches of opponents were as fully and promptly reported as his own. Able men—and the province could boast then of an extraordinary number of really able men—gathered round him or sent contributions to the paper, while from all parts of the country came correspondence, telling Mr Howe what was going on. As he began to feel his powers, and to know that he had power in reserve; to hold his own with older and better educated men; and to taste the sweets of popular applause, that fame which he, like all young poets, had affected to despise appeared beautiful and beckoned him onwards.

He loved his country from the first, and, as it responded to him, that love increased, until it became one of his chief objects to excite in the bosoms of the people the attachment to the soil that gave them birth, which is the fruitful parent of the virtues of every great nation.

To promote this object he made sacrifices. He published, between 1828 and 1839, ten volumes, connected with the history, the law, and the literature of the province, often at his own risk. Another of his literary enterprises was the formation of 'The Club,' a body composed of a number of friends who met in Howe's house, discussed the questions of the day, and planned literary sketches, afterwards published in the *Nova Scotian*. Among those who thus gathered round him, such men as S. G. W. Archibald, Beamish Murdoch, and Jotham Blanchard are now only remembered by students of Nova Scotian history. Even the Irish wit and humour of Laurence O'Connor Doyle gives him but a local immortality. But the names of Thomas C. Haliburton (Sam Slick) and Captain John Kincaid of the Rifle Brigade are known even to superficial students of English literature, and no two men were more regular members of 'The Club.'

Literary rambles and literary sketches were all very well, but what really roused enthusiasm in those days was the political struggle. 'Poetry was the maiden I loved,' said Howe in after years, 'but politics was the harridan I married.' In the early nineteenth century aristocracy and democracy, alike in politics and in society, were fighting their battle all over Europe, and the struggle had spread to the British colonies. In the first year of his editorship Howe had a little brush with the lieutenant-governor and his circle, but not for some time did the crisis come. On the 1st of January 1835 an anonymous letter appeared in the *Nova Scotian* criticizing the financial administration of the city of Halifax and impugning the integrity of its administrators. Howe as editor was responsible. With his trial for criminal libel, and his speech in his defence, his real political life begins.

CHAPTER III
THE OLD COLONIAL SYSTEM

To understand the system of government which Howe assailed, we must go back to the very origin of the British colonies. In the sixteenth and seventeenth centuries an exaggerated importance was attached to money as such. A dollar's worth of gold or silver was held to be of more value than a dollar's worth of grain or timber; not merely more convenient, or more portable, or more easily exchangeable, but absolutely of more value. A country was supposed to be rich in proportion to the amount of money or bullion which it possessed. At first the only colonies prized were those which, like the Spanish, sent bullion to the mother country. Later on, when it was found that bullion need not be brought directly into a country, but might come in the course of trade, this exaggerated belief in money compelled the mother country so to regulate the trade of the colonies as to increase her stores of bullion. To keep as much money as possible within the Empire the colonies were compelled to buy their manufactures in the mother country, and as far as possible to restrict their productions to such raw materials as she herself could not produce, and which she would otherwise be compelled to buy from the foreigner. In carrying out this policy the mother country did her best to be fair; the relation was not so much selfish as maternal. If the colonies were restricted in some ways, they were encouraged in others. If, for example, Virginia was forbidden manufactures, her tobacco was admitted into Great Britain at a lower rate of duty than that of Spain or other foreign countries, and tobacco-growing in England was forbidden altogether.

This system, which was embodied in a series of Acts known as Acts of Trade, or Navigation Acts, did not, in the state of development they had reached, hurt the colonies. In some ways it was actually of advantage to them. A new country, with cheap land and dear labour, must always devote itself mainly to the production of raw materials, and to many of these colonial raw materials Great Britain gave a preference or bounties. At the same time, as was only natural, the tendency was for the colonies to look on the advantages as no more than their due, and on the restrictions as selfish and unjustifiable.

Though attempting thus to regulate the economic development of the colonies, the mother country paid little attention to their political growth. There was indeed in each colony a governor, sent out from England, and a Council, which was supposed to help him in legislation and in government; but more and more power passed, with but little resistance from Great Britain, into the hands of an Assembly elected by the people of the colony. As one Loyalist wrote of them, the Assembly soon discovered 'that themselves were the substance, and the Governor and Board of Council were shadows in their political frame.'

At the American Revolution the revolutionary leaders were, in the main, men of the people, trained in political arts and eloquence in these local assemblies; their complaints against the mother country were, in part at least, against her restrictive colonial system. Hence, after the winning of American independence, when the mother country endeavoured to draw lessons from her defeat, it appeared to her statesmen that the colonies had been lost through too much political democracy in them and too much economic control by her. Thus after the Revolution we find a series of favours given to colonial trade. The timber trade and the shipbuilding of Nova Scotia were aided by bounties and preferential duties. Her commerce was still largely with Great Britain, where she purchased manufactured articles, though even here certain concessions were made; but so important were the favours considered that not even Howe thought the control a grievance, and when in 1846-49 Great Britain inaugurated free trade and put the colonies upon their own feet, Nova Scotians, while not despairing as openly as did the people of Montreal, yet thought it a very great blow indeed.

While conferring these favours, Great Britain exercised a growing control over Nova Scotian political affairs. The Assembly, granted in 1758, was indeed retained, but a restraining hand was kept on it by the Colonial Office in London, through the governor and the Council. An attempt was made to combine representative and irresponsible government. The House of Assembly might talk, and raise money, but it did not control the expenditure, the patronage, or the administration, and it could neither make nor unmake the ministry. The more important House was the Council, which consisted of twelve gentlemen appointed by the king, and holding their offices practically for life. This body was at once the Upper House of the Legislature, corresponding to our present Senate, and the Executive or Cabinet. It was also to a certain extent a judicial body, being the Supreme Court of Divorce for the province. It sat with closed doors, admitting no responsibility to the people. Yet no bill could pass but by its consent. It discharged all the functions of government; all patronage was vested in it. It might do these things ill; its administration might be condemned by every one of the representatives of the people; but its authority remained unaffected.

In this Council sat the heads of departments, as they do in our modern Cabinet. They were appointed in and by Great Britain, and helped to control the commercial policy. Another member was the bishop of the Anglican Church, for the seemly ceremonies and graded orders of clergy of this body were deemed to be a counterpoise to popular vagaries and vulgarity. Prior to the American Revolutionary War there had been no colonial bishopric; three years after its close the first bishop of Nova Scotia was appointed.

Owing to the favour shown to this Church, education long remained almost entirely in its hands, and to the political struggle an element of religious bitterness was added. King's College at Windsor, at first the only institution of higher learning in the province, was not open to any person who should 'frequent the Romish mass, or the meeting houses of Presbyterians, Baptists, or Methodists, or the conventicles or places of worship of any other dissenters from the Church of England, or where divine service shall not be performed according to the liturgy of the Church of England.' It is true that the Church enjoyed no rights which she did not at the time enjoy in England, and that King's College was less illiberal than were the Universities of Oxford and Cambridge; but the circumstances were widely different. In England the Anglicans comprised the bulk of the people, and almost the whole of the cultivated and leisured classes; in Nova Scotia they were in the minority. Yet when, in 1820 and again in 1838, an attempt was made to found Dalhousie College at Halifax on a more liberal basis, the opposition of the Church of England led to the failure of the scheme.

In the Council the chief justice had a seat. As a member of the Legislature he made the law; as one of the Executive he administered the law; and as judge he interpreted the law.

But the most potent element in the Council was for some time the bankers. Early in the nineteenth century, when there was no bank in the province, the government had issued notes, for the redemption of which the revenues of the province were pledged. In 1825 some of the more important merchants founded a bank, and issued notes payable in gold, silver, or provincial paper. The Halifax Banking Company, as this institution was called, was simply a private company, with no charter from the province, and that it was allowed to issue notes is an instance of the easy-going ways of those early days. No less than five of its partners were members of the Council. Thus the state of affairs for some years was that there was but one bank in the province, that its notes were redeemable in provincial paper, and that the Council was largely composed of its directors, who could order the province to print as much paper as they wished!

The Halifax Banking Company was of great benefit to the provincial merchants, and, though its partners made large profits, there is no proof that they abused their position on the Council to aid them in business. But the general feeling in the province was one of suspicion, and the combination of financial and legislative monopoly was certainly dangerous. Soon some other citizens endeavoured to found another bank and to have it regularly incorporated by provincial charter, with the proviso that all paper money issued by it should be redeemable in coin. The directors of the Halifax Banking Company fought this proposal fiercely, both in business circles and in the Council, arguing that as the balance of trade was against Nova Scotia, there would rarely be enough 'hard money' in the province to redeem the notes outstanding. In 1832, however, popular clamour forced the legislature to grant its charter to the second bank, the Bank of Nova Scotia. The Halifax Banking Company[1] also continued to do a flourishing business, and during the struggle of Howe and his fellow-reformers against the Council, the influence of its partners was one of the chief causes of complaint.

Thus the Council comprised the leaders in Church and State, among them the chief lawyers and business men. These formed the 'Society' of Halifax, and to them were added the government officials, who were usually appointed from England. Some of the latter were men of honour and energy, but others were mere placemen in need of a job. When the famous Countess of Blessington wished to aid one of her impecunious Irish relations, she had only to give a smile and a few soft words to the Duke of Wellington, and her scape-grace brother found himself quartered for life upon the revenues of Nova Scotia. Charles Duller, in his pamphlet *Mr Mother Country of the Colonial Office*, hardly exaggerated when he said that 'the patronage of the Colonial Office is the prey of every hungry department of our government. On it the Horse Guards quarters its worn-out general officers as governors; the Admiralty cribs its share; and jobs which even parliamentary rapacity would blush to ask from the Treasury are perpetrated with impunity in the silent realm of Mr Mother Country. O'Connell, we are told, after very bluntly informing Mr Ruthven that he had committed a fraud which would forever unfit him for the society of gentlemen at home, added, in perfect simplicity and kindness of heart, that if he would comply with his wishes and cease to contest Kildare, he might probably be able to get some appointment for him in the colonies.'

When the governor came out entirely ignorant of colonial conditions he naturally fell under the influence of those with whom he dined, and as all dealings with the British government were carried on through him, the Council and the officials had by this means the ear of the Colonial Office. An office-holding oligarchy thus grew up, with traditions and prestige, and known, as in Upper Canada, by the name of the 'Family Compact.' Nowhere did this system seem so strong as in Nova Scotia; nowhere did its leaders show so much ability or a higher sense of honour; nowhere did they endeavour to govern the province in so liberal a spirit. Yet it was fundamentally un-British, and it was to be completely overthrown by the attack of a printer's boy turned editor.

The leaders of the Family Compact in Nova Scotia were not only men of ability and integrity, they had also a reasoned theory of government. Their ablest exponent of this theory and the stoutest defender of the old system was Thomas Chandler Haliburton, Howe's lifelong personal friend and political antagonist.

Haliburton was at once a scholar and a wit. In 1829 Howe published for him his *Historical and Statistical Account of Nova Scotia*, a work which, in spite of its mistakes, may still be read with profit. In 1836-37 a series of sketches appeared in the *Nova Scotian*, which were reprinted with the title of *The Clockmaker; or the Sayings and Doings of Sam Slick of Slickville*. These were issued in volume form in 1837, and took by storm the English-speaking world. The book has no plot. It tells how the author and his friend Sam, a shrewd vulgar Down-East Yankee, ride up and down the province discoursing on anything and everything. Shrewd, kindly, humorous, with an unfailing eye for a pretty woman or a good horse, selling his clocks by 'a mixture of soft sawder and human natur',' so keen on a trade that he will make a bad bargain rather than none at all, yet so knowing that he almost always comes out ahead, Sam is real to the finger-tips. From Haliburton flows the great stream of American dialect humour. Mark Twain, Artemus Ward, and a dozen others, all trace their descent from him.

But Haliburton's real object was intensely serious. He desired to awake Nova Scotians from their lethargy. 'How much it is to be regretted,' he wrote, 'that, laying aside personal attacks and petty jealousies, they would not unite as one man, and with one mind and one heart apply themselves sedulously to the internal improvement and development of this beautiful province. Its value is utterly unknown, either to the general or local government.' It is in his writings that we find the best exposition and defence of the 'Compact' theory of government.

'Responsible Government,' says Haliburton, 'is responsible nonsense.' Some one must be supreme, and as between colony and mother country, it must be the latter. The governor is sent out by the Colonial Office, and to that office he must be responsible. Were he responsible to his ministers or to the local House of Assembly, he might have to act in a way displeasing to the mother country, and subordination would be at an end. Responsible Government is a form of government only fit for an independent country. It is incompatible with the colonial status.

But not only was Responsible Government impossible for a colony; it would, in any case, be a bad system for Nova Scotia, because it would be too democratic. A wise constitution must be, like that of Great Britain, composed of various elements. Such a mixed constitution Nova Scotia had. The governor contributed a bit of Monarchy, the Council a bit of Aristocracy, the Assembly a bit of Democracy. All had thus their fair share. Under Responsible Government, with all power in the hands of the Legislative Assembly, the balance would be overthrown and the democracy would be supreme. To Haliburton, control by the democracy meant control by the crafty, self-seeking professional politician, as he saw him, or thought he saw him, in the neighbouring United States. The people, well meaning, but ignorant and greedy, were at the mercy of the appeals to prejudice and pocket of these wily knaves. Government should be the affair of the enlightened minority, placed, as far as might be, in a position of security and freedom from temptation. This government would not be perfect, for 'power has a natural tendency to corpulency,' but it would be far superior to an unbridled democracy.

THOMAS CHANDLER HALIBURTON.
From an engraving in the Dominion Archives

Speaking of the tree of Liberty, which had grown so splendidly in the United States, Haliburton makes an American say to Sam: 'The mobs have broken in and torn down the fences, and snapped off the branches, and scattered all the leaves about, and it looks no better than a gallows tree.' Let the people attend to business, build their railways, develop their water-powers, their farms, and their forests, secure under the fostering care of the select few. 'I guess if they'd talk more of *rotations* and less of *elections*, more of them ar *dykes* and less of *banks*, and attend more to *top-dressing* and less to *re-dressing*, it 'ed be better for 'em.... Members in general ain't to be depended on, I tell you. Politics makes a man as crooked as a pack does a pedlar, not that they are so awful heavy, neither, but it teaches a man to stoop in the long run.'

Such, then, was the system and theory of government in Nova Scotia. Well defended as it was, it had one fundamentally weak point: the people of Nova Scotia did not want it. Howe had no great regard for the professional politician, whether in the legislature or in the village store. 'Rum and politics are the two curses of Nova Scotia,' he said. But he saw that it would be absurd to tell the people to let well enough alone, when, rightly or wrongly, they were discontented with their government. The way to put an end to hectic agitation was not to curse or to satirize poor human nature, but to remove the cause of the agitation.

From early days there had been struggles against the oligarchy. In 1830 the speaker of the House, S. G. W. Archibald, protested against an attempt of the Council to lower the duty on brandy. Apart from the evident desire of the great merchants on the Council to get brandy in cheap and sell it dear, he took his stand on the fundamental maxim that taxation was the affair of the people's House alone, that there should be 'no taxation without representation.' A man is not necessarily a village politician because he lives in a village, or a great statesman because the stage on which he struts is wide. In this petty scuffle in an obscure colony were involved the same principles on which John Hampden defied King Charles. The Council gave way, and the old system went on as before.

Then, on the 1st of January 1835, a letter appeared in the *Nova Scotian*, accusing the magistrates of Halifax of neglect, mismanagement, and corruption, in the government of the city. No names were mentioned; the tone was moderate; but the magistrates were sensitive and prosecuted Howe for libel. At this time there was not an incorporated city in any part of the province. All were governed by magistrates who held their commission from the Crown. When Howe received the attorney-general's notice of trial, he went to two or three lawyers in succession, and asked their opinion. They told him that he had no case, as no considerations were allowed to mitigate the severe principle of those days, that 'the greater the truth the greater the libel.' He resolved to defend himself. The next two weeks he gave up wholly to mastering the law of libel and the principles upon which it was based, and to selecting his facts and documents. With his head full of the subject, and only the two opening paragraphs of his speech written out and committed to memory, he faced the jury. He had spoken before, but only to small meetings, and on no subjects that touched him keenly. Now the Court House was crowded, popular sympathy entirely on his side, and the real subject himself. That magic in the tone that gives a vibrating thrill to an audience sounded for the first time in his voice. All eyes turned to him; all faces gleamed on him; he noticed the tears trickling down one old gentleman's cheeks; he received the sympathy of the crowd, and without knowing gave it back in eloquence. He spoke for six hours and a quarter, and though the chief justice adjourned the court to the next day, the spell was unbroken. He was not only acquitted, but borne home in triumph on the shoulders of the crowd, the first, but by no means the last, time that such an extremely inconvenient honour was paid him by the Halifax populace. When once inside his own house, he rushed to his room and, throwing himself on his bed, burst into passionate weeping—tears of pride, joy, and overwrought emotion—the tears of one who has discovered new founts of feeling and new forces in himself.

On that day the editor leaped into fame as an orator. Early in the next year (1836) the House of Assembly was dissolved. Howe and his friend William Annand were chosen as the Liberal candidates for the county of Halifax, and were elected by large majorities. On taking his seat Howe was at once recognized as the leader of the party, and without delay began the fight.

[1] In 1872 it obtained a charter from the Dominion, but in 1903 was absorbed by the Canadian Bank of Commerce.

CHAPTER IV
THE FIGHT FOR RESPONSIBLE GOVERNMENT

One of the oldest political struggles in the world is that of the people to control their government. In this struggle the barons faced King John at Runnymede. In this struggle King Charles I was sent to the block. It is a struggle of which the end is not yet. In the eighteenth and early nineteenth centuries the British people worked out what seemed to them a satisfactory solution of the problem, by making the Executive, or Government, responsible to the House of Commons, which in its turn had at certain periods to appeal to the people in a general election.

In this system the Executive holds office just so long as it can obtain the support of a majority in the House of Commons. Thus, while certain members of the Executive may be chosen from the House of Lords or the Legislative Council or the Senate or whatever the Upper House may be called, most of its members must sit in the House of Commons, in order to explain or defend their policy. From this arrangement certain consequences follow.

(1) To be endurable a government must be more or less permanent, must have time to initiate and, partly at least, to carry out its policy. Constantly shifting governments would be intolerable. But if the government depends on the will of a majority, then that majority must also be more or less permanent. Hence we get the party system, by which the House of Commons is divided into two parties, each with a coherent policy. The leaders of the party which has the majority at the general election form the Executive, or Government, and, if they can keep their majority together, these leaders hold office till the people pronounce their verdict at the next general election.

(2) Members of a party will only work together under their leaders if those leaders have a coherent policy on which they agree, and which wins the sympathy of their followers. 'It doesn't matter much what we say, gentlemen,' said a British prime minister to his colleagues on a famous occasion, 'but we must all say the same thing.' Once a government under this system has made up its mind, each member must sink his individual opinion, or must resign.

(3) But while the Cabinet as a body must 'say the same thing,' its members must also be heads of departments, for the competent administration of which they are responsible. One man must have charge of the Customs, another of Finance, another of Justice, and so on.

This system of heads of departments, each responsible for his own branch, but all uniting in a common responsibility for the common policy, and holding office at the will of a majority in the House of Commons, is known as Responsible Government. Under it the sovereign, as has been said, 'reigns but does not govern.' The monarch of England acts only on the will of his advisers. Once the Cabinet has decided, and has had its decision ratified by a majority in the two Houses of Parliament, the monarch has no choice but to obey. Dignified and honourable functions the Crown still has; but in administration the ultimate decision rests with the ministers. 'In England the ministers are king,' said a European monarch.

To every man alike in Great Britain and in the colonies this form of government seemed, as has been said, fit only for an independent nation, and inconsistent with the colonial status. To Howe it was the essential birthright of British freemen, and he determined to vindicate it for his native province.

But Howe was no doctrinaire, bound at all costs to uphold a system. He was a practical man, fighting practical abuses. When parliament met, early in 1837, the young editor, already recognized as the Liberal leader, in company with Laurence O'Connor Doyle, began the fight by bringing in a resolution against the practice of the Council of sitting with closed doors. To this the Council replied that such a matter of procedure concerned themselves alone. Howe replied by introducing into the Assembly a series of twelve resolutions, embracing a general attack on the Council for its secrecy, its irresponsibility, and its ecclesiastical and social one-sidedness, and ending by an appeal to His Majesty 'to take such steps as will ensure responsibility to the Commons.' Eloquent though his speech was in defence of these resolutions, he showed that he did not yet see the line along which salvation was to come. 'You are aware,' he said, 'that in Upper Canada an attempt was made to convert the Executive Council into the semblance of an English ministry, having its members in both branches of the legislature, and holding their positions while they retained the confidence of the country. I am afraid that these colonies, at all events this province, is hardly prepared for the erection of such machinery: I doubt whether it would work well here: and the only other remedy which presents itself is, to endeavour to make both branches of the legislature elective.' Howe had thus diagnosed the disease, but he was inclined to prescribe an inadequate and probably harmful remedy.

The debate on the twelve resolutions was hot. On the question of opening the doors of the Council, Howe had been unanimously followed, but his general attack on that body roused strong feelings among its friends and adherents in the Assembly, and though all his resolutions were passed, on each vote there was a resolute minority. Yet the debate, though hot, was on a high level, and does credit to the political capacity and the sense of decorum of early Nova Scotia.

The Council were prompt to take up the gage of battle. A day or two after their receipt of the resolutions they returned a message which ignored eleven of the twelve, but insisted on the rescinding of the one which spoke of the disposition of some of their members 'to protect their own interests and emoluments at the expense of the public.' They hinted in unmistakable terms that, unless this was rescinded, they would refuse to concur in a bill for voting supply. Their refusal to do so would have meant that, while they were prepared to vote public funds to pay the salaries of the officials, they would hold up all grants for roads, bridges, education, and other public needs.

Great was the consternation. The members of the majority in the House of Assembly saw themselves in anticipation compelled to appear before their constituents and explain that they had been unable to vote this money because they had joined with a pestilent young editor in an attack on his elders and betters.

Howe sat up all night wondering what he should do. Then he determined to take his medicine like a man. On the next day he entered the House with cheerful face and buoyant step. He threw back his coat, a gesture already growing familiar, and stood four-square to the Assembly. 'I feel,' he said, 'that we have now arrived at a point which I had to a certain extent anticipated from the moment I sat down to prepare the resolutions ... the position in which we are now placed does not take me by surprise.... But it may be said, What is to be done? And I answer, Sacrifice neither the revenue nor the cause of reform. In dealing with an enemy who is disposed to take us at disadvantage, like politic soldiers, let us fight with his own weapons.... The Council ask us to rescind a particular resolution; I am prepared to give more than they ask and to rescind them all.... But I shall follow up that motion by another, for the appointment of a committee to draw up an address to the Crown on the state of the Colony.... It is not for me to say, when a committee is appointed, what the address shall contain; but I presume that having these resolutions before them, and knowing what a majority of this Assembly think and feel, they will do their duty, and prepare such a document as will attain the objects for which we have been contending.'[1]

A motion to rescind the twelve resolutions followed and was carried, and the revenues were saved. Before the end of the session Howe's thinking had advanced, and the address to the Crown which his committee prepared implored the monarch either 'to grant us an elective Legislative Council; or to separate the Executive from the Legislative Council, providing for a just representation of all the great interests of the province in both; and, by the introduction into the former of some members of the popular branch and otherwise securing responsibility to the Commons, confer upon the people of this province what they value above all other possessions, the blessings of the British constitution.'

Lord Glenelg, at this time the colonial secretary, was a weak but amiable man. He could not see that in the full grant to the colonies of Responsible Government lay safety; he deemed it 'inconsistent with a due adherence to the essential distinctions between a Metropolitan and a Colonial Government.[1] But he was a kindly soul, who was honestly shocked at the predominance in the Council of the Church of England and the bankers, and he went as far as he dared. In August 1837 dispatches from him arrived, directing the lieutenant-governor to separate the Legislative and the Executive Councils. Of the wisdom of this step he was by no means sure, but he yielded to the wish of the Assembly, 'convinced that their advice will be dictated by more exact and abundant knowledge of the wants and wishes of their constituents than any other persons possess or could venture to claim.' In the new Executive Council the chief justice was not to sit, and the banking and Church of England influences were to be lessened. The Council of Twelve thus became an Executive merely, while a new Legislative Council, or Upper House, of nineteen members, came into being. Though no responsibility to the Commons was acknowledged, and though 'the Queen can give no pledge that the Executive Council will always comprise some members of the Assembly,' four members of the new Executive did actually sit in the Lower House and three in the Upper. Already the fortress was giving way. Instead of finding out the policy of the Executive by an elaborate interchange of written communications, the Assembly could now, whenever it so desired, interrogate such members of the Executive as were chosen from its own body.

Towards the end of this year broke out the rebellion headed in Lower Canada by Papineau and in Upper Canada by William Lyon Mackenzie. Its ignominious failure threatened for a time to overwhelm Howe with charges of similar disloyalty. Luckily he had in 1835 written to Mr H. S. Chapman, a prominent Upper Canadian Reformer, a long letter in which, while sympathizing with the grievances of the Reformers, he had indignantly denounced any attempt to use force, and had vindicated the loyalty of Nova Scotia. This letter he now published, and triumphantly cleared his character.

The rebellion had at least the merit of awakening the British government. When houses went up in smoke, when Canadians with fixed bayonets chased other Canadians through burning streets and slew them as they cried for mercy, the most fat-hearted place-man could not say that all was for the best in the best of all possible colonies. The British government sent out as High Commissioner one of England's ablest men, Lord Durham. His report, published early in 1839, is a landmark in the history of British colonial administration. Disregarding all half-measures, he declared that in Responsible Government alone could salvation for the colonies be found. In clarion tones he proclaimed that thus alone could the deep, pathetic, and ill-repaid loyalty of the Canadas be preserved. But the report had still to be acted on. Lord John Russell, the ablest man in the government, had succeeded Lord Glenelg, and in 1839 he made a speech which did indeed mark an advance on the views of his predecessor, but which fell far short of the wishes of the Canadian Reformers. The internal government of the province, he admitted, must be carried on in accordance with the well-understood wishes of the Canadian people, but he still held Responsible Government to be incompatible with the colonial status. The governor of a colony can be responsible, he said, only to the Crown; to make him responsible to his ministers would be to proclaim him head of an independent state. If the governor must act on the advice of his ministers, he might be forced to choose ministers whose acts would embroil the province, and thereby the whole Empire, with a foreign power.

In answer to this speech Howe wrote to Lord John Russell four open letters, which were republished in almost every Canadian newspaper, and which, issued in pamphlet form, were sent to every British newspaper and member of parliament. Never did he reach a higher level. Vigorous, sparkling, full of apt illustration and sound political thought, they grip 'little Johnny Russell's' speech and shake it to tatters. 'By the beard of the prophet!'—to use one of Howe's favourite oaths—here is a big man, a man with a gift of expression and a grip of principle. They should be read in full, for an extract gives but a truncated idea of their power.

He ridicules the arrogation to itself by the 'Compact' of a monopoly of loyalty. 'It appears to me that a very absurd opinion has long prevailed among many worthy people on both sides of the Atlantic: that the selection of an Executive Council, who, upon most points of domestic policy, will differ from the great body of the inhabitants and the majority of their representatives, is indispensable to the very existence of colonial institutions; and that, if it were otherwise, the colony would fly off, by the operation of some latent principle of mischief, which I have never seen very clearly defined. By those who entertain this view, it is assumed that Great Britain is indebted for the preservation of her colonies, not to the natural affection of their inhabitants—to their pride in her history, to their participation in the benefit of her warlike, scientific, or literary achievements—but to the disinterested patriotism of a dozen or two of persons, whose names are scarcely known in England, except by the clerks in Downing Street; who are remarkable for nothing above their neighbours in the colony, except perhaps the enjoyment of offices too richly endowed; or their zealous efforts to annoy, by the distribution of patronage and the management of public affairs, the great body of the inhabitants, whose sentiments they cannot change.'[2]

He applies Lord John's reasoning to the British towns of London or Glasgow or Aberdeen, and shows what absurd results it would produce. He admits fully that Nova Scotia cannot be independent, and that there are limits beyond which, were her responsible Executive mad enough to pass them, the governor might rightly interpose his veto. But he shows in what a fiasco any such situation would necessarily end. The powers which he leaves to the British government would now, indeed, be thought excessive.

'From what has been already written, it will be seen that I leave to the Sovereign and to the Imperial Parliament the uncontrolled authority over the military and naval force distributed over the colonies; that I carefully abstain from trenching upon their right to bind the whole empire by treaties and other diplomatic arrangements with foreign states; or to regulate the trade of the colonies with the mother country and with each other. I yield to them also the same right of interference which they now exercise over colonies and over English incorporated towns; whenever a desperate case of factious usage of the powers confided, or some reason of state, affecting the preservation of peace and order, call for that interference.'[3]

But he pleads eloquently that the loyalty of Nova Scotia need not be maintained by sending over to govern her a well-intentioned military man, gallant and gouty, with little knowledge of her history or her civil institutions, with a tendency to fall under the control of a small social set, whose interests are different from or adverse to those of the great majority; that it will only strike deeper root if the governor is given as his advisers not such an irresponsible council, but the popular leaders, men strong in the confidence of the province.

Events moved rapidly. In October 1839 Lord John Russell sent out to the governors of the various British North American colonies a circular dispatch of such importance that it was recognized by Sir John Harvey, the governor of New Brunswick, as 'a new and improved constitution.' In this it was said that 'the governor must only oppose the wishes of the Assembly where the honour of the Crown, or the interests of the Empire, are deeply concerned,' and office-holders were warned that they were liable to removal from office 'as often as any sufficient motives of public policy may suggest the expediency of that measure.' A subsequent paragraph stated clearly that this was not meant to introduce the 'spoils system,' but to apply only to the heads of departments and to the other members of the Executive Council.

Sir Colin Campbell, at this time lieutenant-governor of Nova Scotia, was a very gallant soldier of unstained honour and kindly disposition, a personal friend of the Duke of Wellington, under whom he had proved his valour in India and in the Peninsula. When in 1834 an epidemic of cholera ravaged Halifax, Sir Colin went down into the thick of it, and worked day and night to assuage the distressing agonies of the sufferers. In politics, however, he was under the sway of the Council. He now refused to communicate Lord John Russell's dispatch to the House, and when that body passed a vote of want of confidence in the Executive, Sir Colin met them with a curt reply to the effect that 'I have had every reason to be satisfied with the advice and assistance which they [the Executive] have at all times afforded me.'

But 'there was the sound of a going in the tops of the mulberry trees.' Mr J. B. Uniacke rose in the House and stated that, in the conviction of the absurdity of the present irresponsible system, he had tendered to the governor his resignation as an Executive Councillor. Mr Uniacke, a man of fine presence, oratorical gifts, and high social position, had hitherto been the Tory leader and Howe's chief opponent in the House, and his conversion to the side of Responsible Government was indeed a triumph. But there was fierce work still to do. By a large majority the House passed an address to the governor expressing unfeigned sorrow at his refusal to administer the government in accordance with Lord John Russell's dispatch. To this Sir Colin replied that the matter was of too great moment for him to decide, and that he would refer it to Her Majesty's government. This in effect meant that he would spin the affair out for another six months or so, and so shift the burden of decision to his successor. The patience of the House was at an end, and an address to the Crown was passed, detailing the struggle and requesting 'Your Majesty to remove Sir Colin Campbell and send to Nova Scotia a governor who will not only represent the Crown, but carry out its policy with firmness and good faith.'

To ask Her Majesty to remove her representative was an extreme measure. From one end of the province to the other meetings were held. With one antagonist after another Howe crossed swords, and was ever victorious. Lord Sydenham, the governor-general, who though resident in Canada had authority over all British North America, came down to Halifax to look into the matter. He had a long talk with Howe and each yielded to the charm of the other. Such warm friends did they become that during the rest of Sydenham's short life they exchanged frequent letters, and Howe called one of his sons by the name of Sydenham. In September 1840 Lord Falkland was sent out as lieutenant-governor, Sir Colin Campbell having been 'promoted' to the governorship of Ceylon. It is pleasant to think of the old soldier's last meeting with Howe. Passing out from Lord Falkland's first levee, Howe bowed to Sir Colin and would have passed on. The veteran stopped him, and held out his hand, exclaiming, 'We must not part in this way, Mr Howe. We fought out our differences of opinion honestly. You have acted like a man of honour. There is my hand.' The hand was warmly grasped, and on Sir Colin's departure a fine tribute to his chivalry and sense of honour was paid by the *Nova Scotian*.

With the coming of Lord Falkland the first stage in the struggle was over. That nobleman endeavoured to carry out in Nova Scotia the policy of Lord Sydenham in Canada and to remain in a half-way house. Greatly to their rage, four members of the Executive Council, who held seats in neither branch of the legislature, were at once informed that their services could no longer be retained. Three of the places so vacated were given to Uniacke, Howe, and a third Liberal, and it was agreed that other Liberals should be brought into the Executive Council as vacancies occurred.

This account gives but a poor idea of the excitement in Halifax during these years. In so small a community, where every one knew every one else, personal, social, and political questions became hopelessly intertwined. The fighting was bitter. 'Forced into a cleft stick, there was nothing left for us but to break it,' was Howe's pithy way of putting the case. Naturally enough, the stick objected to being broken. And as in every war, for one man killed in battle five or six die from other causes connected with the war—bad boots, bad food, bad rum, wet clothes, the trenches for beds, hospital fever, and such like—so the open opposition of debate was the least that Howe had to fear. That, as one of the finest peasantry in the world said of Donnybrook, 'was enjoyment.' Howe was once asked by an old sportsman, with whom he had gone fishing for salmon, how he liked that sport. 'Pretty well,' was the answer; 'but, after all, it's not half so exciting as a fortnight's debate in the Legislature, and a doubt as to the division.' The personal slanders in private circles—and he could not afford to be wholly indifferent to them; the misrepresentation not only of motives, but of the actual objects sought to be attained, which circulate from mouth to mouth till they become the established 'they say' of society; those ceaseless petty annoyances and meannesses of persecution which Thackeray declares only women are capable of inflicting; these were showered about and on him like a rain of small-shot, and they *do* gall, no matter how smilingly a man may bear himself. After all, these people did as most of us would probably have done. They were taught, and they believed easily, that the printer Howe was bad, that he spoke evil of dignitaries, that he was a red republican, and a great many other things equally low. The dignitaries could not control themselves when they had to refer to him; to take him down to the end of a wharf and blow him away from a cannon's mouth into space was the only thing that would satisfy their ideas of the fitness of things. Their women, if they saw him passing along the street, would run from the windows shrieking as if he were a monster whose look was pollution. Their sons talked of horse-whipping, ducking in a horse-pond, fighting duels with him, or doing anything in an honourable or even semi-honourable way to abate the nuisance. Nor did they confine themselves to talk. On one occasion, before Howe became a member of the House, a young fellow inflamed by drink mounted his horse and rode down the street to the printing-office, with broadsword drawn, declaring he would kill Howe. He rode up on the wooden sidewalk, and commenced to smash the windows, at the same time calling on Howe to come forth. Howe, hearing the clatter, rushed out. He had been working at the case, and his trousers were bespattered with ink and his waistcoat was only half buttoned. He appeared on the doorstep with bare head and shirt-sleeves partly rolled up, just as he had been working, and took in the situation at a glance. He did not delay a minute or say a word. His big white face glowed with passion, and going up to the shouting creature he caught him by the wrist, disarmed and unhorsed him, and threw him on his back in a minute. Some years later another young man challenged Howe to a duel. Howe went out, received his fire, and then fired in the air. He was challenged afterwards by several others, but refused to go out again. And he was no coward. There was not a drop of coward's blood in his body. Even a mob did not make him afraid. Once, when the 'young Ireland' party had inflamed the Halifax crowd against him, he walked among them on election day as fearlessly as in the olden time when they were all on his side. He knew that any moment a brickbat might come, crushing in the back of his head, but his face was cheery as usual, and his joke as ready. He fought as an Englishman fights: walking straight up to his enemy, looking him full in the face, and keeping cool as he hit from the shoulder with all his might. And when the fighting was over, he wished it to be done with. 'And now, boys,' said he once to a mob that had gathered at his door, 'if any of you has a stick, just leave it in my porch for a keepsake.' With shouts of laughter the shillelaghs came flying over the heads of the people in front till the porch was filled. The pleasantry gave Howe a stock of fuel, and sent away the mob disarmed and in good humour.

We can see the true resolve that was in such a man, but those who fought hand to hand with him may be excused if they could not see it. He was the enemy of their privileges, therefore of their order, therefore of themselves. It was a bitter pill to swallow when a man in his position was elected member for the county. The flood-gates seemed to have opened. Young gentlemen in and out of college swore great oaths over their wine, and the deeper they drank the louder they swore. Their elders declared that the country was going to the dogs, that in fact it was no longer fit for gentlemen to live in. Young ladies carried themselves with greater hauteur than ever, heroically determined that they at least would do their duty to Society. Old ladies spoke of Antichrist, or sighed for the millennium. All united in sending Howe to

Coventry. He felt the stings. 'They have scorned me at their feasts,' he once burst out to a friend, 'and they have insulted me at their funerals!'

When Uniacke left the Tory camp, his own friends and relatives cut him in the street. When Lord Falkland requested the resignations of the four irresponsible councillors, their loyalty to the Crown did not restrain their attacks upon himself. His sending his servants to a concert was spoken of as a deliberate insult to the society of Halifax; and his secretary was accused of robbing a pawnbroker's shop to replenish his wardrobe.

There was too much of human nature in Joe Howe to take all this without striking hard blows in return. He did strike, and he struck from the shoulder. He said what he thought about his opponents with a bluntness that was absolutely appalling to them. He went straight to the mark aimed at with Napoleonic directness. They were stunned. They had been accustomed to be treated so differently. Hitherto there had been so much courtliness of manner in Halifax; the gradations of rank had been recognized by every one; and the great men and the great women had been treated always with deference. But here was a Jacobin who changed all this; who in dealing with them called a spade a spade; who searched pitilessly into their claims to public respect, and if he found them impostors declared them to be impostors; and who advocated principles that would turn everything upside down.

Lord Falkland was a well-meaning young nobleman of great good looks and small political experience. His ruling characteristic was pride. Shortly before leaving Halifax he had his carriage-horses shot, lest on his departure they should fall into plebeian hands. His hauteur was fortified by his wife, daughter by a morganatic marriage of King William IV. Could such a man carry through a compromise, by which men of opposite views should sit in his Cabinet? In Canada it had taken all the skill and political experience of Lord Sydenham; under Sir Charles Metcalfe the new wine burst the old bottles, bespattering more than one reputation in the process. That the new governor would soon take offence at the jovial, self-confident, free manners of Howe was almost certain.

The new Executive Council was a compromise. Prime minister there was none. Its head was still the governor, whom Howe himself admitted to be 'still responsible only to his sovereign.' On the question which in Canada brought about the quarrel between Sir Charles Metcalfe and his advisers, Howe said in 1840 that in Nova Scotia 'the patronage of the country is at his [the governor's] disposal to aid him in carrying on the government.' In 1841 he still accorded him the initiative, saying that 'the governor, as the Queen's representative, still dispenses the patronage, but that as the Council are bound to defend his appointments, the responsibility even as regards appointments is nearly as great in the one case as in the other.'

During these years Howe had a delicate role to play. The extreme and logical members of his own party attacked him as a trimmer; on the other hand, any one of the four extruded councillors was considered by Society to be worth a hundred Howes, and Society was not slow to make its feelings known. The fight was fiercest in the Executive Council, where the party of caution, if not of reaction, was led by the Hon. J. W. Johnston. Tall and distinguished in appearance, with dark flashing eyes and imperious temper, of fine probity in his private life, and with a keen, though somewhat lawyer-like, intellect, Johnston was no unworthy antagonist to the great tribune of the people. Though of good birth, and recognized in Society as Howe was not, he was a Baptist, and so not hampered in the popular mind by any connection with the official Church. Nor were his views on government illiberal. The controversy between him and Howe was rather of temperament than of principles, between the keen lawyer, mistrustful of spontaneity, lingering fondly over his precedents, and the impulsive, over-trustful, over-generous lover of humanity. In the working out of the new system anomalies soon developed, which Falkland was not the man to minimize. Howe himself was still a little misty in his views, and accepted the speakership as well as a seat in the Executive Council, thus becoming at once umpire and participant, a position impossible to-day. In the next year, however, he resigned the speakership to accept the post of collector of customs for Halifax.

But the great wrangle was over the extent to which Responsible Government had been conceded. One member of the government said that 'Responsible Government was responsible nonsense—it was independence. It would be a severing of the link which bound the colony to the mother country.' Johnston, at the time sitting in the Upper House, did not go so far, but said that 'in point of fact it is not the intention to recognize the direct responsibility which has been developed in the address. To concede such would be inconsistent with colonial relations.' There was no fundamental discrepancy between Johnston's views and those of Howe. Later on in the same speech, Johnston, while considering the subject to be 'incapable of exact definition,' yet said that 'the change simply is that it becomes the duty of the representative of Her Majesty to ascertain the wishes and feelings of the people through their representatives, and to make the measures of government conform to these so far as is consistent with his duty to the mother country.' This is really much the same as Howe's statement that 'the Executive, which is to carry on the administration of the country, should sympathize with to a large extent, and be influenced by, and when proper be composed of to a certain degree, those who possess the confidence of the country'; especially when this is taken in connection with his other statement that he had no wish for colonial assemblies 'to interfere in the great national regulations, in arrangements respecting the army or navy of the Empire, or the prerogatives of the parliament or Crown.' But the emphasis was different. Howe insisted on the greatness of the change in local administration; Johnston on the amount of still surviving control by the mother country. The little rift in the lute was already apparent, and was increased by the natural tendency of the governor to consult the courtly Johnston, and to show impatience at the brusque familiarity of Howe.

The tension became greater and greater. There is no reason to doubt that both Howe and Johnston tried to play the game. But their temperaments and their associates were different, and they grew more and more mistrustful of each other. Accusations of treachery began to fly. By the autumn of 1842 Howe had ceased to disguise his 'conviction that the administration, as at present constituted, cannot go on a great while longer.' The final break-up came over the question of education. It is sad that this should have been so, for Howe well knew that education should bring peace and not a sword. We may make education a battle-ground,' he said, 'where the laurels we reap may be wet with the tears of our country.' At this time primary education was optional, given in private schools, aided in some cases by provincial grants. Both Howe and Johnston would fain have substituted a compulsory system, supported by local assessments, but both feared the repugnance of the country voters to direct taxation, and it was not till 1864 that Dr (afterwards Sir) Charles Tupper took this fearless and notable step forward. In the mean time both Howe and Johnston supported the increase of grants to education, the establishment of circulating libraries, and the appointment of a superintendent of education.

But if schools were too few, universities were too many, and it was here that the quarrel began. King's College at Windsor was avowedly Anglican. An attempt had been made in 1838 to revive Dalhousie as undenominational, but the bigotry of Sir Colin Campbell and of a rump board of governors under Presbyterian influence refused to appoint as professor the Rev. Dr Crawley, on the almost openly avowed ground that he was a Baptist. The aggrieved denomination then hived off, and started at Wolfville their own university, known as Acadia. The Roman Catholics had for some time had in operation St Mary's College at Halifax. All these received grants from the government, and were endeavouring to do university work in a very imperfectly educated community of three hundred thousand people.

Theoretically this system was absurd. But each of the little colleges had its band of devoted adherents, held fast to it by the strongest of all ties, that of religion. Most of all was this the case with Acadia, founded in hot and justifiable anger, and eager to justify its existence. Had Howe been a wary politician, he would have thought twice before stirring up such a wasp's nest, more especially as the Baptists had hitherto been his faithful supporters. But Howe was both more and less than a wary politician, and when early in 1843 a private member brought in resolutions in favour of withdrawing the grants from the existing colleges, and of founding 'one good college, free from sectarian control, and open to all denominations, maintained by a common fund,' Howe supported him with all his might. In thus differing from his colleagues on a question of primary importance he was undoubtedly guilty of ignoring the doctrine of collective Cabinet responsibility.

The heather was soon on fire. Johnston came vigorously to the rescue of Acadia. The Baptist newspaper attacked Howe in no measured terms. Crawley himself in public speeches endeavoured to show 'the extreme danger to religion of the plan projected by Mr Howe of one college in Halifax without any religious character, and which would be liable to come under the influence of infidelity.' Howe repaid invective with invective. 'I may have been wrong, but yet when I compare these peripatetic, writing, wrangling, grasping professors, either with the venerable men who preceded them in the ministry of their own Church, or in the advent of Christianity, I cannot but come to the conclusion that either one set or the other have mistaken the mode. Take all the Baptist ministers from one end of the province to the other—the Hardings, the Dimocks, the Tuppers,—take all that have passed away, from Aline to Burton; men who have suffered every privation, preaching peace and contentment to a poor and scattered population; and the whole together never created as much strife, exhibited so paltry an ambition, or descended to the mean arts of misrepresentation to such an extent, in all their long and laborious lives, as these two arrogant professors of philosophy and religion have done in the short period of half a dozen years.'[4]

In reply to Dr Crawley he contrasted the students of an undenominational college, 'drinking at the pure streams of science and philosophy,' with the students of Acadia 'imbibing a sour sectarian spirit on a hill.' 'It is said, if a college is not sectarian, it must be infidel. Is infidelity taught in our academies and schools? No; and yet not one of them is sectarian. A college would be under strict discipline, established by its governors; clergymen would occupy some of its chairs; moral philosophy, which to be sound must be based on Christianity, must be conspicuously taught; and yet the religious men who know all this raise the cry of infidelity to frighten the farmers in the country.'

Johnston, in evident alarm at the success of Howe's agitation, persuaded the governor to dissolve the House and hold a general election. At the same time he himself, with great courage, resigned his life-membership of the Legislative Council, and offered himself as a candidate for the Assembly. A hot election followed, in which both Howe and Johnston were returned at the head of approximately equal numbers.

By this time Howe had learned his lesson. A half-way house might be a useful stopping-place, but could not be a terminus. A unanimous Cabinet was a necessity, and a unanimous Cabinet was possible only if backed by a unanimous party. He therefore offered Lord Falkland either to resign, or to form a Liberal administration from which Johnston and those who thought with him should be excluded. This Lord Falkland could not see, nor yet could Johnston. The latter 'unequivocally denounced the system of a party government, and avowed his preference for a government in which all parties should be represented.' At last, on Falkland's urgent request, Howe consented to remain in the government till the House met. A few days later the governor suddenly appointed to the Executive Council Mr Almon, a high Tory and Johnston's brother-in-law. It was too much; Howe and his Liberal colleagues at once resigned.

Was he in the right? With Almon as a man they had no quarrel. Howe and Johnston were both well qualified to serve their native province. Why should one consume his energy in trying to keep out the other? The answer is that a government is not merely composed of heads of separate departments. It is a unity, responsible for a coherent policy, and as such cannot contain two men, however estimable, who differ on political fundamentals. It is Howe's merit that he saw this, while Johnston and Falkland did not. After all, their loud cries for a non-party administration only meant an administration in which their own party was supreme. Howe was wholly in the right when he said that Johnston's epitaph should be, 'Here lies the man who denounced party government, that he might form one; and professing justice to all parties, gave every office to his own.'

There followed three years of hard fighting. Johnston formed an administration, which was sustained by a majority varying from one to three. Debates of thirteen and fourteen days were common. Howe's relations with Lord Falkland had at first been those of intimate friendship, and for a time the quarrel was conducted with decorum. Several months after his resignation he could write, 'personal or factious opposition to your Lordship I am incapable of.' But a literary gentleman, in close connection with Lord Falkland, began in the press a series of fierce attacks on Howe and the other Liberal leaders. Of Lord Falkland's sanction and approval there could be little doubt. His Lordship himself said in private conversation that between him and Howe it was 'war to the knife,' and personally denounced him in his dispatches to the Colonial Office. Howe was not the man to refuse such a challenge. Though retaining his seat in the House, he resumed the editorship of the *Nova Scotian*, which he had abandoned in 1841. From his editorial chair he not only guided the parliamentary Opposition, but pelted the governor himself with a shower of pasquinades in prose and verse. Lord Falkland has practically put himself at the head of the Tory party, said Howe, and as a political opponent he shall have no mercy. A flood of Rabelaisian banter was poured upon the head of the unhappy nobleman. He was attacked in his pride, his tenderest place. It is impossible not to wish that Howe had shown more moderation. He had, of course, precedent on his side. Nothing which he wrote was so bad as the language of Queen Elizabeth to her councillors, or of Frederick the Great to Voltaire. He was neither more savage than Junius, nor more indecent than Sir Charles Hanbury Williams in his attacks on King George II. But times had changed. Mouths and manners had grown cleaner, and much of Howe's banter is over-coarse for present-day palates. But of its effectiveness there is no doubt. He fairly drove the unhappy Falkland out of the province. After all, his raillery was an instrument in the fight for freedom, and a less deadly one than the scythes and muskets of Mackenzie or Papineau.

A squib which produced much comment in its day was 'The Lord of the Bedchamber,' which begins thus:

The Lord of the Bedchamber sat in his shirt,
(And D—dy the pliant was there),
And his feelings appeared to be very much hurt
And his brow overclouded with care.

It was plain, from the flush that o'ermantled his cheek,
And the fluster and haste of his stride,
That, drowned and bewildered, his brain had grown weak
By the blood pumped aloft by his pride.

So it goes on, not unamusing, full of topical allusions and bad puns. The serious Johnston, with some lack of humour, brought the matter up in the House, and came near to accusing Howe of High Treason. Howe wisely refused to take the matter seriously, and defended himself in a speech of which a fair sample is: 'This is the first time I ever suspected that to hint that noblemen wore shirts was a grave offence, to be prosecuted in the High Court of Parliament by an Attorney General. Had the author said that the Lord of the Bedchamber wore no shirt, or that it stuck through his pantaloons, there might have been good ground of complaint.' On the more serious question he said: 'The time has come when I must do myself justice. An honest fame is as dear to me as Lord Falkland's title is to him. His name may be written in Burke's Peerage; mine has no record but on the hills and valleys of the country which God has given us for an inheritance, and must live, if it lives at all, in the hearts of those who tread them. Their confidence and respect must be the reward of their public servants. But if these noble provinces are to be preserved, those who represent the sovereign must act with courtesy and dignity and truth to those who represent the people. Who will go into a Governor's Council if, the moment he retires, he is to have his loyalty impeached; to be stabbed by secret dispatches; to have his family insulted; his motives misrepresented, and his character reviled? What Nova Scotian will be safe? What colonist can defend himself from such a system, if a governor can denounce those he happens to dislike and get up personal quarrels with individuals it may be convenient to destroy?'[5]

In 1846 the quarrel came to a crisis. The speaker of the House and his brother, a prominent member of the Opposition, were connected with an English company formed for building Nova Scotian railways. To the astonishment of everybody, a dispatch from Lord Falkland to the Colonial Office was brought down and read before the speaker's face, in which his own name and that of his brother were repeatedly mentioned, and in which they were held up to condemnation as the associates of 'reckless' and 'insolvent' men. Howe was justly indignant at this gross breach of constitutional procedure, and indeed of ordinary good manners. Leaping to his feet, he said: 'I should but ill discharge my duty to the House or to the country, if I did not, this instant, enter my protest against the infamous system pursued (a system of which I can speak more freely, now that the case is not my own), by which the names of respectable colonists are libelled in dispatches sent to the Colonial Office, to be afterwards published here, and by which any brand or stigma may be placed upon them without their having any means of redress. If that system be continued, some colonist will, by and by, or I am much mistaken, hire a black fellow to horsewhip a lieutenant-governor.'[6]

In reply to a vote of censure by the House, he defended himself in a letter to his constituents, of which the pith is in the final sentences: '"But," I think I hear some one say, "after all, friend Howe, was not the supposititious case, which you anticipated might occur, somewhat quaint and eccentric and startling?" It was, because I wanted to startle, to rouse, to flash the light of truth over every hideous feature of the system. The fire-bell startles at night; but if it rings not the town may be burned; and wise men seldom vote him an incendiary who pulls the rope, and who could not give the alarm and avert the calamity unless he made a noise. The prophet's style was quaint and picturesque when he compared the great king to a sheep-stealer; but the object was not to insult the king, it was to make him think, to rouse him; to let him see by the light of a poetic fancy the gulf to which he was descending, that he might thereafter love mercy, walk humbly, and, controlling his passions, keep untarnished the lustre of the Crown. David let other men's wives alone after that flight of Nathan's imagination; and I will venture to say that whenever, hereafter, our rulers desire to grille a political opponent in an official dispatch, they will recall my homely picture and borrow wisdom from the past.'[7]

Later in the year Lord Falkland was recalled, and appointed governor of Bombay. Soon afterwards Howe wrote to a friend: 'Poor Falkland will not soon forget Nova Scotia, where he learned more than ever he did at Court. I ought to be grateful to him, for but for the passages of arms between us, there were some tricks of fence I had not known. Besides, I now estimate at their true value some sneaking dogs that I should have been caressing, for years to come, and lots of noble-hearted friends that only the storms of life could have taught me adequately to prize.'

SIR JOHN HARVEY.
From a portrait in the John Ross Robertson Collection, Toronto Public Library

Falkland's successor was Sir John Harvey, in old days a hero of the War of 1812, more recently governor of New Brunswick. Shortly after his coming he endeavoured to induce Howe and his friends to enter the government, but Howe now saw victory within his grasp, and had no mind for further coalitions. To a friend he wrote: 'I do not in the abstract disapprove of coalitions, where public exigencies, or an equal balance of parties, create a necessity for them, but hold that, when formed, the members should act in good faith, and treat each other like gentlemen—should form a party, in fact, and take the field against all other parties without. If they quarrel and fight, and knock the coalition to smithereens, then a governor who attempts to compel men who cannot eat together, and are animated by mutual distrust, to serve in the same Cabinet, and bullies them if they refuse, is mad.'

Foiled in his well-meant attempt, Sir John then consulted the Colonial Office. Into that department a new spirit had come with the arrival in 1846 of Lord Grey, who replied with a dispatch in which the principles of Responsible Government were laid down in the clearest terms, while at the same time the Reformers were warned that only the holders of the great political offices should be subject to removal, and that there should be no approach to the 'spoils system,' which was at the time disgracing the United States. In 1847 the Reformers carried the province, and Sir John Harvey gave to their leaders his loyal support. Mr Uniacke was called on to form an administration, in which Howe was given the post of provincial secretary. There was a final flurry. For a month or two the province was convulsed by the conduct of the former provincial secretary, Sir Rupert D. George, who, amid the plaudits of fashionable Halifax, refused to resign. But Sir Rupert was dismissed with a pension, and Joe Howe ruled in his stead. The ten years' conflict was at an end. The printer's boy had faced the embattled oligarchy, and had won.

It was a bloodless victory. Heart-burning indeed there was, and the breaking up of friendships. But it is the glory of Howe that responsibility was won in the Maritime Provinces without rebellion. In the next year, in his song for the centenary of the landing of the Britons in Halifax, he exultantly broke out:

The blood of no brother, in civil strife poured,
In this hour of rejoicing encumbers our souls!
The frontier's the field for the patriot's sword,
And cursed is the weapon that faction controls!

In conclusion we must ask ourselves, was it worth while? Was the winning of Responsible Government a good thing? We are apt to take this for granted. Too many of our historians write as if all the members of the Family Compact had been selfish and corrupt, and all our present statesmen were altruistic and pure. Both propositions are equally doubtful. A man is not necessarily selfish and corrupt because he is a Tory, nor altruistic and pure because he calls himself a Liberal or a Reformer. It is very doubtful whether Nova Scotia is better governed to-day than it was in the days of Lord Dalhousie or Sir Colin Campbell. Native Nova Scotians have shown that we do not need to go abroad for lazy and impecunious placemen. But two things are certain. Nova Scotia is more contented, if not with its government, at least with the system by which that government is chosen, and it has within itself the capacity for self-improvement. Before Joseph Howe Nova Scotians were under tutors and governors; he won for them the liberty to rise or fall by their own exertions, and fitted them for the expansion that was to come.

[1] The full text of this speech will be found in Chisholm, *Speeches and Letters*, vol. i, p. 144.

[2] Chisholm, *Speeches and Letters*, vol. i, p. 223.

[3] Chisholm, *Speeches and Letters*, vol. i, p. 252.

[4] Chisholm, *Speeches and Letters*, vol. i, p. 432.

[5] Chisholm, *Speeches and Letters*, vol. i, p. 531.

[6] Chisholm, *Speeches and Letters*, vol. i, p. 594.

[7] Chisholm, *Speeches and Letters*, vol. i, p. 600.

CHAPTER V
RAILWAYS AND IMPERIAL CONSOLIDATION

In 1825 a train of cars, carrying coal, drawn by a steam locomotive, ran from Stockton to Darlington in Lancashire. In a week the price of coals in Darlington fell from eighteen shillings to eight shillings and sixpence. In 1830 the 'Rocket,' designed by George Stephenson, ran from Liverpool to Manchester at a rate of nearly forty miles an hour, and the possibilities of the new method of transportation became manifest. But the jealousy of the landed interest, eager to maintain the beauty and the privacy of the countryside, retarded till the forties the growth of English railways. Meanwhile, by the use of railways the United States altered her whole economic life and outlook. In 1830 she had twenty-three miles of railway, five years later over a thousand, and by 1840 twenty-eight hundred miles; and thereafter till 1860 she almost doubled her mileage every five years.

In the meantime Canada lagged behind, though in no other country were the steel bands eventually to play so important a part in creating national unity. The vision of Lord Durham first saw what the railway might do for the unification of British North America. 'The formation of a railroad from Halifax to Quebec,' he wrote in 1839, 'would entirely alter some of the distinguishing characteristics of the Canadas.' Even before this, young Joseph Howe had seen what the steam-engine might do for his native province, and in 1835 he had advocated, in a series of articles in the *Nova Scotian*, a railway from Halifax to Windsor. Judge Haliburton was an early convert; and in 1837 he makes 'Sam Slick' harp again and again on the necessity of railways. 'A railroad from Halifax to the Bay of Fundy' is the burden of many of Sam's conversations, and its advantages are urged in his most racy dialect. But the world laughed at Haliburton's jokes and neglected his wisdom. Though in 1844 the British government directed the survey of a military road to unite Nova Scotia, New Brunswick, and Quebec, and though in 1846 the three provinces joined to pay the expenses of such a survey, which was completed in 1848, British North America was for the ten years which followed Lord Durham's Report too busy assimilating his remedy of Responsible Government to have much energy left for practical affairs. But in 1848, along with the triumph of the Reformers alike in the Canadas, New Brunswick, and Nova Scotia, railways succeeded Responsible Government as the burning political question, and to no man did their nation-building power appeal with greater force than to Howe.

Already he had witnessed one proof of the power of steam. In 1838, in company with Haliburton, he was on his way to England on the *Tyrian*, one of the old ten-gun brigs which carried the mails, slow and uncomfortable at the best, unseaworthy death-traps in a storm. As she lay rolling in a flat calm with flapping sails, a few hundred miles from England, a smear appeared on the western horizon. The smear grew to a smudge, the smudge to a shape, and soon there steamed up alongside the *Sirius*, a steamer which had successfully crossed the Atlantic, and was now on her return to England. The captain of the *Tyrian* determined to send his mails on board. Howe accompanied them, took a glass of champagne with the officers, and returned to the brig. Then the *Sirius* steamed off, leaving the *Tyrian* to whistle for a breeze. On their arrival in England, Howe and Haliburton succeeded in combining the chief British North American interests in a letter to the Colonial Office. That much-abused department showed sympathy and promptitude. Negotiations were entered into, contracts were let, and in 1840 the mails were carried from England to Halifax by the steamers of a company headed by Samuel Cunard, a prominent Halifax merchant, founder of the line which still bears his name. At once the distance from England to Nova Scotia was reduced from fifty days to twelve. Certainty replaced uncertainty; danger gave way to comparative security. It was the forging of a real link of Empire.

A decade later Howe saw that the railway could play the same part. At this time the question was being discussed in all the provinces. Nova Scotia wished to link her harbours with the trade of the Canadian and American West and of the Gulf of St Lawrence, so as to be at least the winter port of the northern half of North America. New Brunswick wished to give to the fertile valley of the St John and the shores of the Bay of Fundy an exit to the sea, and to unite them with the American railways by a line from St John to Portland. The need of Canada was still more pressing; between 1840 and 1850 she had completed her St Lawrence system of canals, only to find them side-tracked by American railways. A line from Montreal to Windsor, opposite Detroit, became a necessity.

It is characteristic of Howe that he was at first attracted by the thought of what might benefit Nova Scotia, and that he gradually passed from this to a great vision of Empire, in which his early idea was absorbed though not destroyed. His first speech on the subject was delivered on the 25th of March 1850, and is chiefly notable for his strong advocacy of government construction. In July a convention to discuss the matter was called at Portland, to which the Nova Scotian government sent a more or less official representative. This gathering passed resolutions in favour of a line from Portland to Halifax through St John. But Maine and Portland had no money wherewith to build, and the British provinces could not borrow at less than six per cent, if at that. Howe had not been present at Portland, but he was the leader at an enthusiastic Halifax meeting in August, which voted unanimously in favour of government construction of a line from Halifax to the New Brunswick boundary, to connect with whatever line that province should build. Later in the year he was sent by his government as a delegate to Great Britain, in the endeavour to secure an Imperial guarantee, which would reduce the interest on the money borrowed from six to three and a half per cent. It seemed a hopeless quest. Earl Grey, who at the time presided over the Colonial Office, was a strong believer in private enterprise, and was opposed to government interference. In July he had returned a curt refusal to Nova Scotia's request. But Howe had a strong and, as the result proved, a well-founded belief in his own powers of persuasion.

His visit was a triumph, or rather a series of triumphs. Landing early in November, he had several interviews with Lord Grey, and with the under-secretary, Mr Hawes. On the 25th of November 1850 he addressed to Grey a long and forcible open letter, in which he urged the claims of Nova Scotia. A month later he was met with a refusal. But Howe knew that there were ways and means of bringing a government office to terms. He had friends in Southampton, and at once arranged with them that a spontaneous request to address the citizens of that town should come to him from the city authorities. Then he wrote to Lord Grey and requested an interview. The reply came that 'His Lordship will be glad to see Mr Howe on Monday.' Howe's comment in his private diary is as follows:

'Will he, though? He would be glad if I were with the devil, or on the sea with Hawes's note [of refusal] sticking out of my pocket. We shall see. Head clears, as it always does when the tug of war approaches. To-morrow must decide my course, and we shall have peace and fair treatment, or a jolly row. Message from Hawes: "Don't despair." Never did: What does the under-secretary mean? If kindness and rational expectations, it is well; if more humbug, the hardest must fend off.'

His account of the interview is given in his diary: 'Letters from home; thank God, all well, but evidently anxious. I am glad they do not know how this day's work may affect their fortunes. Read letters and papers and try to divert myself till hour for interview comes.

'It comes at last: a thousand thoughts go rushing through my brain as, with a scowling brow and infernal mental struggle to control my passions, I ride, smoking, down to Downing Street. To be calm and good-natured, even playful, down to the last, is my policy; to hint at my resources without bullying and menace will be good taste. The Ante-Room, the Abomination of Desolation. Enter Mr Howe at last, Earl Grey and Mr Hawes looking very grim and self-complacent. Two to one is long odds. But here goes at you: "Ye cogging Greeks, have at ye both." The interview lasted two hours. What passed may be guessed by the result. When I entered the room, my all trembled in the balance. When I came out, Hawes had his letter of the 28th in his pocket, it being suppressed and struck off the files. I had permission to go my own way and finish my case before any decision was given. I had, besides, general assurances of sympathy and aid, and permission to feel the pulse of the public in any way I pleased. Viva! "Boldness in civil business," says old Bacon, but as I go down Downing Street my heart is too full of thankfulness to leave room for any throb of triumph.'

Thus his threat to appeal from Downing Street to parliament and people had won; but could he win before the people? On the 14th of January he faced a crowded meeting at Southampton, which grew more and more enthusiastic as he went on. Two days later he addressed another open letter to Lord Grey, the result of six weeks' hard labour, during which, he says, 'it seemed to me that I had read a cart-load and written a horse-load.' Three times was it copied before he had it to his satisfaction. The draft was carefully gone over by Lord Grey, who suggested certain excisions and additions. Both of his open letters and his Southampton speech were widely circulated, and attracted great attention. Howe's name was on every lip. His praises were sung by members of both parties in the House of Lords. After some delay, due to a reorganization of the government, on the 10th of March he received a formal letter from Mr Hawes, of which not only Lord Grey and himself but also the Cabinet had already seen and approved the draft, pledging the credit of the British government to the extent of seven million pounds to an intercolonial railway uniting Canada, New Brunswick, and Nova Scotia. Very few conditions were attached. As Howe said on his return to Nova Scotia: 'She virtually says to us by this offer, There are seven millions of sovereigns, at half the price that your neighbours pay in the markets of the world; construct your railways; people your waste lands; organize and improve the boundless territory beneath your feet; learn to rely upon and to defend yourselves, and God speed you in the formation of national character and national institutions.'[1]

What were the arguments by which Howe brought about this great reversal of policy? Though knowing Grey to be opposed to the general principle of public ownership, he began by singing its praises. The best road is the queen's highway. The toll-bar and the turn-pike are disappearing. 'All our roads in Nova Scotia, made by the industry and resources of the people, are free to the people at this hour.' The railway should be built with the same ideal. 'If our government had means sufficient to build railroads and carry the people free, we believe that would be sound policy.' This being impossible, government ownership would at least keep down the rates, and save the people from the private greed which was at the time so manifest in the conduct of English lines.

He then went on to show with a wealth of statistics that Nova Scotia was thoroughly solvent, and that the Imperial guarantee was almost certain never to be called on. This done, he turned gladly to the constitutional side. That the road would pay, he believed; but he advocated it not as a 'paying proposition,' but as a great link of Empire. British North America must be united, and must be given a place in the Empire. At present the colonial is doomed to a colonial existence. 'The North American provinces must,' he wrote to Grey, 'either:

Be incorporated into the Realm of England,

Join the American Confederacy,

Be formed into a nation.

If the first can be accomplished, the last may be postponed indefinitely, or until all parties are prepared for it. If it cannot, Annexation comes as a matter of course. To avert it is the duty of Englishmen, on both sides of the Atlantic.' It rests with Great Britain to say which road British North America is to take. 'The higher paths of ambition, on every hand inviting the ardent spirits of the Union, are closed to us. From equal participation in common right, from fair competition with them in the more elevated duties of government and the distribution of its prizes, our British brethren on the other side as carefully exclude us. The president of the United States is the son of a schoolmaster. There are more than one thousand schoolmasters teaching the rising youth of Nova Scotia with the depressing conviction upon their minds that no very elevated walks of ambition are open either to their pupils or their own children.... Suppose that, having done my best to draw attention to the claims of those I have the honour to represent, I return to them without hope; how long will high-spirited men endure a position in which their loyalty subjects their mines to monopoly, their fisheries to unnatural competition, and in which cold indifference to public improvement or national security is the only response they meet when they make to the Imperial authorities a proposition calculated to keep alive their national enthusiasm, while developing their internal resources?'[2] There is a balance of power in Europe which British diplomacy labours incessantly to maintain. Each possible transfer of a few acres of ground by some petty German princeling is carefully studied by the Foreign Office. Is the creation of a power in North America to balance the United States to be forever considered of no importance? Nova Scotia especially, whose praises he sings with lusty eloquence, has been unfairly treated. As the result of a rebellion which cost the mother country millions, Canada had been granted a large loan. Nova Scotia had kept loyal; had put every man and every dollar in the province at the service of her sister province of New Brunswick, when trouble with the United States over the boundary seemed near. Yet she had received no loan;

instead, she had been burdened by the grant to an English company of the monopoly of her coal areas.

Then he turns to the subject of emigration, at the time much in the public eye, and shows how superior is British North America to Australia, then highly spoken of. He paints vividly the heart-rending poverty of the British lower classes, and the fertility of the acres waiting to receive them.

'Whence come Chartism, Socialism, O'Connor land-schemes, and all sorts of theoretic dangers to property, and prescriptions of new modes by which it may be acquired? From this condition of real estate. The great mass of the people in these three kingdoms own no part of the soil, have no bit of land, however small, no homestead for their families to cluster round, no certain provision for their children.

'A new aspect would be given to all the questions which arise out of this condition of property at home, if a wise appropriation were made of the virgin soil of the Empire. Give the Scotchman who has no land a piece of North America, purchased by the blood which stained the tartan on the Plains of Abraham. Let the Irishman or the Englishman whose kindred clubbed their muskets at Bloody Creek, or charged the enemy at Queenston,[3] have a bit of the land their fathers fought for. Let them have at least the option of ownership and occupation, and a bridge to convey them over. Such a policy would be conservative of the rights of property and permanently relieve the people. It would silence agrarian complaint and enlarge the number of proprietors.'[4]

To convey such emigrants, to give them work, to find them markets, the railway was a necessity. To bring them over he urged government supervised and subsidized steamers, 'the Ocean omnibus.'

These ideas he developed on his return to Halifax in one of the noblest of his speeches. 'But, sir, daring as may appear the scope of this conception, high as the destiny may seem which it discloses for our children, and boundless as are the fields of honourable labour which it presents, another, grander in proportions, opens beyond; one which the imagination of a poet could not exaggerate, but which the statesman may grasp and realize, even in our own day. Sir, to bind these disjointed provinces together by iron roads; to give them the homogeneous character, fixedness of purpose, and elevation of sentiment, which they so much require, is our first duty. But, after all, they occupy but a limited portion of that boundless heritage which God and nature have given to us and to our children. Nova Scotia and New Brunswick are but the frontage of a territory which includes four millions of square miles, stretching away behind and beyond them to the frozen regions on the one side and to the Pacific on the other. Of this great section of the globe, all the northern provinces, including Prince Edward Island and Newfoundland, occupy but 486,000 square miles. The Hudson's Bay territory includes 250,000 square miles. Throwing aside the more bleak and inhospitable regions, we have a magnificent country between Canada and the Pacific, out of which five or six noble provinces may be formed, larger than any we have, and presenting to the hand of industry and to the eye of speculation every variety of soil, climate, and resource. With such a territory as this to overrun, organize, and improve, think you that we shall stop even at the western bounds of Canada, or even at the shores of the Pacific? Vancouver's Island, with its vast coal measures, lies beyond. The beautiful islands of the Pacific and the growing commerce of the ocean are beyond. Populous China and the rich East are beyond; and the sails of our children's children will reflect as familiarly the sunbeams of the South as they now brave the angry tempests of the North. The Maritime Provinces which I now address are but the Atlantic frontage of this boundless and prolific region— the wharves upon which its business will be transacted and beside which its rich argosies are to lie. Nova Scotia is one of these. Will you then put your hands unitedly, with order, intelligence, and energy, to this great work? Refuse, and you are recreants to every principle which lies at the base of your country's prosperity and advancement; refuse, and the Deity's handwriting upon land and sea is to you unintelligible language; refuse, and Nova Scotia, instead of occupying the foreground as she now does, should have been thrown back, at least behind the Rocky Mountains. God has planted your country in the front of this boundless region; see that you comprehend its destiny and resources—see that you discharge with energy and elevation of soul the duties which devolve upon you in virtue of your position. Hitherto, my countrymen, you have dealt with this subject in a becoming spirit, and, whatever others may think or apprehend, I know that you will persevere in that spirit until our objects are attained. I am neither a prophet nor a son of a prophet, yet I will venture to predict that in five years we shall make the journey hence to Quebec and Montreal and home through Portland and St John, by rail; and I believe that many in this room will live to hear the whistle of the steam-engine in the passes of the Rocky Mountains and to make the journey from Halifax to the Pacific in five or six days.'[5]

The question of the future of British North America had long occupied his mind. His first recorded speech was a call to young Nova Scotians to raise their province to a place amid the nations of the earth. The easy patronage of Englishmen, whose intellectual equal he knew himself to be, roused him the more because he felt it to be in a sense justified. America by rebellion had risen to manhood; was Nova Scotia by loyalty to be doomed to inferiority? At first independence attracted him, but by the date of his letters to Grey he had come to believe in 'annexation to our mother country' as a better choice, though he reiterated that independence would be preferable to the indefinite endurance of the present position. The change might come gradually, but come it must. Colonial regiments; a colonial navy, if only of a few frigates; colonial representation in the Imperial parliament, the colonies sending 'to the House of Commons one, two, or three members of their cabinets, according to their size, population, and relative importance.'

This idea of Imperial Federation goes back to the days before the American Revolution, and was brought in with them by the Loyalists. It was a much greater favourite with the 'Family Compact' than with the Reformers, and was urged alike by John Beverley Robinson in Upper Canada and by Haliburton in Nova Scotia, from whom Howe probably derived it. But though not its originator, Howe was at least its eloquent exponent, and he did much to rouse Nova Scotians to the conviction that some remedy for their inferiority must be found.

At the end of his second letter he boldly speaks in a way which must have endeared him to Lord Grey's heart. The transportation of criminals had long been a recognized part of British policy, but at this time it was breaking down before the growth of the penitentiary system in England and the colonial dislike of the system. South Africa had just been brought to the verge of rebellion by the arrival of a shipload of gallows-birds; armed colonists had forbidden them to land, and very rough messages had been sent home to Lord Grey. It may be imagined with what joy the harassed colonial secretary welcomed a proposal of Howe that selected convicts, confined for light offences, should be lent to Nova Scotia for work under military supervision along the more unsettled portions of the line. Their continuance in the country was evidently expected, for Howe said: 'If a portion of comparatively wilderness country were selected for the experiment, the men might have sixpence per day carried to their credit from colonial funds while they laboured, to accumulate till their earnings are sufficient to purchase a tract of land upon the line, with seed and implements to enable them to get a first crop when the period of service had expired.'[6]

To this Grey replied that while no convicts would be sent unless definitely asked for by a colonial government, in that event a moderate number would be provided 'without any charge for their custody and subsistence to the province which may have applied for them.' After returning to Nova Scotia Howe defended his proposal, with the express proviso that the safeguards were sufficiently strict; but the experience of other countries tends to show that the idea was dangerous, and that Nova Scotia did well not to act on it.

On his return Howe was at the height of his fame. His mission had been successful beyond the dreams of the most sanguine. His quick dramatic temper thrilled to the core at his reception. 'The father, in classic story, whose three sons had gained three Olympic prizes in the same day, felt it was time to die. But, having gained the confidence of three noble provinces, I feel it is time to live.'

'It is clear that, unless done by the government, these great railways cannot be done at all. Even if companies could make them, they would cost fourteen millions instead of seven. But, sir, what is a government for, if it is not to take the lead in noble enterprises; to stimulate industry; to elevate and guide the public mind? You seat eight or nine men on red cushions or gilded chairs, with nothing to do but pocket their salaries, and call that a government. To such a pageant I have no desire to belong. Those who aspire to govern others should neither be afraid of the saddle by day nor of the lamp by night. In advance of the general intelligence, they should lead the way to improvement and prosperity. I would rather assume the staff of Moses and struggle with the perils of the wilderness and the waywardness of the multitude than be a golden calf, elevated in gorgeous inactivity—the object of a worship which debased.'[7]

There were still difficulties to overcome. New Brunswick, though willing to co-operate in his plan, was much more eager for the Portland line, which would run through her settled southern portion and link it with her natural market and base of supplies in the United States. During Howe's absence she had partially committed herself to the construction of such a line by a private company, but Howe was soon able to convert her government to the view that it was better to build both lines with money costing only three and a half per cent than to build one at six per cent. In June her most influential man, Mr Chandler, accompanied Howe to Toronto, where an agreement was soon come to with the Canadian statesmen, of whom the chief was Mr (afterwards Sir) Francis Hincks. In November the Railway Bills were brought down in the Nova Scotian legislature. And then, just when the cup was at Howe's lips, it was dashed from them. A brief dispatch from Lord Grey announced that there had been a misapprehension. The Portland line could not be guaranteed. 'The only railway for which Her Majesty's Government would think it right to call upon Parliament for assistance would be one calculated to promote the interests of the whole British Empire, by establishing a line of communication between the three provinces in North America.' Howe's attempt to have the verdict rescinded led only to its iteration.

The blow fell with crushing force. It was at once obvious that New Brunswick would withdraw from the bargain, and that she would have right on her side in doing so. With the dropping out of the middle section, the intercolonial railway and all that it meant must collapse.

Was success still possible? In January 1852 Hincks and Chandler came to Halifax with a new proposal. If the route could be changed from the Gulf shore to the valley of the St John, New Brunswick would still accept. The change would ensure the support of the southern part of that province, and would also shorten the route to Montreal. Mr Hawes's letter had expressly said that the mother country would not insist on the northern route, if a shorter and better could be found.

The reception of the two representatives was cold. Halifax feared that the proposed route would turn to St John both the grain trade of the west and that of the Gulf of St Lawrence. Howe personally was depressed and sullen. Probably his latent egoism was beginning to show itself. He was asked to sacrifice his scheme, his darling, and to aid in a plan patched up by others. Long conferences were held. Eventually the financial terms were amended in favour of Nova Scotia, and her government, Howe included, gave a somewhat reluctant assent to the new proposal.

A wretched chapter of accidents followed. Early in March Hincks sailed for England; Chandler soon followed; on a series of pretexts Howe delayed his departure. In England, Hincks and Chandler quarrelled with Sir John Pakington, the Conservative mediocrity who had succeeded Grey, and Hincks, brusquely turning his back upon plans of government ownership and control, entered upon negotiations with a great private company which ended in the construction of the Grand Trunk Railway. Of the subsequent series of errors in the financing and building of that line, which left Canadian credit water-logged for thirty years, it is not necessary to speak.[8]

Of this fiasco Howe felt, spoke, and wrote very bitterly. He accused Hincks of having 'ended by throwing our common policy overboard, and rushing into the arms of the great contractors.' Now, it is true that in Halifax in February Hincks had favoured government construction; but he had expressly warned his hearers that if the present plan did not go through, Canada might be compelled to look elsewhere. What Canada most of all desired was connection between Montreal and Portland on the one side and between Quebec and Detroit on the other. For the construction of a 'grand trunk line' running east and west she had already voted several millions. Howe's absence and the quarrel with Pakington had destroyed all hope of success for the government line; instead of crying over spilt milk, Canada must seek a new dairy. Into the question of Hincks's motives or of his financial integrity there is no need to go. The real culprit was Howe, in refusing to help in the final negotiation. He himself has given his defence; it is weak and egoistical. He says that he was worn down by the travel, excitement, and fatigue of the last fifteen months, and that in the depth of winter his opponents forced him to fight a contested election. This might indeed have delayed his departure, while he took a fortnight's holiday; further than that the excuse has no weight. 'Had he gone, he must either have differed from his co-delegates, or have been compromised by their acts. By not going, he left himself free to strike out an independent policy for his own province, when that which had been forced upon Nova Scotia should, as he probably anticipated, have failed.' It is the apology of an egoist. Once again, at Confederation, we shall see him 'striking out an independent policy for his own province,' and with results equally disastrous.

What of his conflict with Lord Grey? On the whole, his Lordship comes out badly. If there is any meaning in words, Mr Hawes had promised that the guarantee should include the Portland line. In the very middle of a paragraph of concessions and stipulations occur the words: 'It is also to be understood that Her Majesty's Government will by no means object to its forming part of the plan which may be determined upon, that it should include a provision for establishing a communication between the projected railway and the railways of the United States.' Grey afterwards stated 'that nothing further was contemplated in that passage than that Her Majesty's Government would sanction such a provision for this purpose as the legislature of New Brunswick may deem expedient to make upon its own liabilities.' A lamer excuse has rarely been penned. The whole letter deals with the guarantee of the British government for 'the plan which may be determined upon,' and neither by word nor by implication gives any countenance to the idea that here in the middle of the paragraph, for one sentence, the idea of an Imperial guarantee is dropped and that of unaided provincial construction substituted.

What was Howe's explanation of his Lordship's tergiversation? It was the same as that which he had for Hincks's *volte-face*. 'A powerful combination of great contractors, having large influence in the Government and Parliament of England, were determined to seize upon the North American railroads and promote their own interests at the expense of the people.' 'If ever all the facts should be brought to light, I believe it will be shown that by some astute manipulation the British provinces on that occasion were sold for the benefit of English contractors and English members of Parliament.'

Put thus crudely the charge is absurd. The reputation of some of the contractors who built the British North American railways is indeed none too good. Howe scarcely exaggerated when he wrote about one of them to the lieutenant-governor that 'in his private offices there is more jobbing, scheming, and corruption in a month than in all the public departments in seven years.' But whatever Lord Grey's mistakes in colonial policy, his long career shows him personally incorruptible, and in some ways almost pedantically high-minded. The charge must be put in another way. Grey was irritable, strong-willed, and inclined to self-righteousness. Nothing is easier than for a self-righteous man to confuse his wishes and his principles. It is probable that he came to feel that Mr Hawes's letter went further than was desirable. To the hot fit induced by Howe's eloquence succeeded cold shivers, which the great contractors naturally encouraged. Of the great firm of Jackson, Peto, Betts, and Brassey, which eventually built the Grand Trunk and the early railways of Nova Scotia and New Brunswick, two at least were influential Whig members of the British House of Commons. Very possibly Lord Grey found that with the Portland guarantee annexed he would have difficulty in forcing the plan through parliament. He may have believed that with the guarantee struck out the provinces would still be able to finance the Portland line. Howe is on sounder lines when he makes the fiasco an argument in favour of his plan of colonial representation in the Imperial parliament. 'The interests of a few members of parliament and rich contractors were on one side, and the interests of the colonists on the other; and in such a case there was no great difficulty in giving two meanings to a dispatch, or in telling a Nova Scotian with no seat in parliament or connections or interest in England that he had made a mistake.

'The Provinces were proceeding to fulfil the conditions, when, unfortunately, two or three members of the Imperial parliament took a fancy to add to the cost of the roads as much more as the guarantee would have saved. It was for their interest that the guarantee should not be given. It was withdrawn. The faith of England—till then regarded as something sacred—was violated; and the answer was a criticism on a phrase—a quibble upon the construction of a sentence, which all the world for six months had read one way. The secret history of this wretched transaction I do not seek to penetrate. Enough is written upon stock-books and in the records of courts in Canada to give us the proportions of that scheme of jobbery and corruption by which the interests of British America were overthrown. But, sir, who believes that if these provinces had ten members in the Imperial parliament, who believes— and I say it not boastingly—had Nova Scotia had but one who could have stated her case before six hundred English gentlemen, that the national faith would have been sullied or a national pledge withdrawn?'[9]

It was the turning-point in Howe's career. For the first time he had attempted Imperial work on a great scale; he had put forward his best powers; and he had failed. His failure wrecked his trust in British and Canadian statesmen, and in the great business interests of England. It did more; it hardened and coarsened his nature. Not that the deterioration was sudden or complete. Some of his most beautiful poetry, some of his finest speeches, were written subsequently. But the weakening had set in, and when in after years he was again called on to face a great crisis, it showed itself with fatal results.

[1] Chisholm, *Speeches and Letters*, vol. ii, p. 169.

[2] Chisholm, *Speeches and Letters*, vol. ii, pp. 113, 115.

[3] See *The War Chief of the Ottawas*, chap. iv, and *The War with the United States*, chap. iv.

[4] Chisholm, *Speeches and Letters*, vol. ii, pp. 130-1.

[5] Chisholm, *Speeches and Letters*, vol. ii, pp. 169-70.

[6] Chisholm, *Speeches and Letters*, vol. ii, p. 140.

[7] Chisholm, *Speeches and Letters*, vol. ii, p. 171.

[8] See *The Railway Builders* in this Series.

[9] Chisholm, *Speeches and Letters*, vol. ii, pp. 289-90.

CHAPTER VI
BAFFLED HOPES

Foiled in the great scheme, the government of Nova Scotia nevertheless went ahead with its policy of provincial railway construction, and in 1854 Howe, to the surprise of many, withdrew from the Executive to accept the post of Railway Commissioner. His motives were probably in part a desire to provide for his family, which his personal extravagance and political honour alike had kept in a continual state of penury, and in part that disgust at partisan bickering which so often seizes upon provincial politicians in their hours of reflection.

He had long had a great desire to enter the Imperial civil service. In the four years between June 1855 and June 1859 the colonies were administered by no less than six secretaries of state: Lord John Russell, Sir William Molesworth, Mr H. Labouchere, Lord Derby, Sir E. Bulwer Lytton, and the Duke of Newcastle. To each of them Howe wrote long letters setting forth his claims to office. To Lord John Russell he says: 'I have exhausted the range of ambitions which that province [Nova Scotia] affords'; and he asks to be made a permanent under-secretary at the Colonial Office, a rank corresponding to the Canadian title of deputy minister. Later in the year, when in London on a provincial mission, he again approached Lord John Russell, writing to him two long letters and having at least one interview. 'A colonial governorship, if there was a vacancy, I would not refuse, but I would prefer employment in your department here, with the hope that I might win my way into parliament, distinguish myself by my pen, or by the intelligent dispatch of public business entrusted to my care.... To win a position here, in the heart of my fatherland, is my highest ambition.' To this Lord John Russell returned the official answer that his claims would be kept in mind.

Later in the year Howe made the same request to Sir William Molesworth. Sir William wrote back a very civil and straight-forward letter, saying that the principle of taking colonials into the Imperial service had just been recognized in the appointment of Mr Hincks to the governorship of Barbados, and that Howe's own claims would be kept in mind, but that 'I have not at present, nor do I see any immediate prospect of my having, any vacancy suitable for you at my disposal either at home or abroad.' Howe naturally viewed with mixed feelings the appointment of his enemy Hincks, and replied: 'If Mr Hincks's appointment be followed up by judicious selection from time to time, as fair opportunities occur, a new spirit will be infused into all the colonies. If it be not, it will only be regarded as an indication of the strength of English combinations which that gentleman has served, and which others, and myself among the number, have not conciliated by the freedom with which we have expressed independent opinions.

'As my letter is to be placed on record, I shall be glad, with your permission, to chiefly found my claim to consideration on the service which I have rendered as the exponent and advocate of the new system of administration that pervades British America, and which we call Responsible Government.'

In 1856 come similar letters to Mr Labouchere; and to Mr Blackwood, a prominent official at the Colonial Office, he thus summarizes his claims: 'I am quite aware that there are many claimants on the patronage of the Crown, and I would not wish importunately to press my own claims. If men of greater worth and capacity are appointed over my head, I trust that I shall have too much good sense and good taste to complain.... I am quite aware that you have many military, naval, and civil officers to provide for, and I am also aware of the advantages which they all possess, in comparison with any colonial gentleman, from being in England or having friends in the House, or elsewhere, to press their claims. As I cannot be on the spot, and have no such aids to rely upon, will you do me the favour, when such matters may be fairly pressed, to urge:

'1. That eighteen years of parliamentary and official life ought to have trained me to comprehend and to administer colonial government.

'2. That mainly by my exertions, the constitution of my native province was remodelled and established upon sound principles.

'3. That a system of public works, devised by me, and now rapidly advancing, is regarded as so important to the prosperity of Nova Scotia and of the provinces generally that all parties acknowledge their value and give me their support.

'4. That, irrespective of colonial interests or feelings, these works, by which troops can be conveyed in a few hours from the depot at Halifax to the Gulf of St Lawrence or Bay of Fundy, and regiments of militia from the eastern and western counties can be concentrated for the defence of its citadel, arsenals, and dockyard, ought to be considered in any comparison in which mere military or naval service may be supposed to outweigh my claims. When completed, these works may fairly be contrasted as a means of defence with all that your engineers have done in the Maritime Provinces for half a century.'

**JOSEPH HOWE.
From a painting by T. Debaussy, London, 1831.
Reproduced in Chisholm's *Speeches and Public Letters of Joseph Howe***

Attempts in 1857 to approach Mr Labouchere through the lieutenant-governor, Sir Gaspard Le Marchant, and through his brother, Sir Denis, a well-known literary man, failed, but in 1858 Lord Derby, whom Howe had known earlier as Lord Stanley, became prime minister, and Howe renewed his claim. With statesmanlike intuition he saw the possibilities of the Pacific slope, now, by the Oregon Treaty, shared between Great Britain and the United States, and asked for the governorship of British Columbia and Vancouver Island, which he thought should be united under the name of British Oregon. Here he could guide the infant steps of a vaster Nova Scotia; here were mountain and valley and sea, farm and forest and fisheries; here were international problems, not only of relations with the United States, but with the awakening East. Lord Derby's answer was delayed, through no fault of his own, and when in November Howe brought out an edition of his collected speeches and public letters, he took advantage of the opportunity to send presentation copies, with long letters, to Lord John Russell, Lord Derby, Sir E. B. Lytton, Mr Merivale, the permanent under-secretary of the Colonial Office, and to several other men of influence. To the colonial secretary he complained bitterly that 'our system denies to a colonist, so trained, the distinctions which others of less experience, with no knowledge of the provinces they are sent to govern, and intellectually not my superiors, readily obtain.' Lord Derby was an English gentleman, and he replied in what Howe himself called 'a very handsome letter,' saying that as he could not interfere with the patronage of the Colonial Office, he had therefore left the matter to Sir E. B. Lytton. 'I regret to find by your letter that you think that you have cause to complain of the conduct of the Colonial Office, in reference to position in the public service.... I am unable to express any opinion upon the subject, except a very confident one that Sir E. Lytton cannot have any disposition to underrate public services, the value of which must be known to all who within the last twenty years have been connected with the North American Colonies.'

Howe's hopes were high. 'I suppose they will now do something with or for me,' he wrote to a friend. But the governorship of British Columbia was not for him. Nor indeed could it be, richly though he had deserved that or any other governorship. The chief interest in the new province was that of the Hudson's Bay Company; for twenty years this company's interests and those of Great Britain had been protected on the Pacific by Sir James Douglas, to whom the governorship rightly fell.

In 1859 Howe made a last appeal to the Duke of Newcastle, with a like result.

It is a sad spectacle, that of the great man knocking at preferment's door, and knocking in vain. Howe was a statesman, with his head full of ideas of Imperial consolidation. His was a great wild heart, deeply touched indeed with ambition, 'the last infirmity of noble minds,' but deeply conscious also of great powers, emotional and intellectual. Small wonder that he raged as he felt that to reach his goal he had to crawl through so narrow a portal, had to abase himself before well-meaning mediocrities like Labouchere or Newcastle.

He could not do it. In none of his letters do we find the real tone of the office-seeker. The man who so haughtily wrote back to Molesworth his opinion of the appointment of Hincks was not the man to commend himself to an official superior. His very merits closed the door against him. Government departments usually prefer to let sleeping dogs lie, to be content with honest administration along existing lines, and to distrust innovation. To bring a new idea into a government department is little less dangerous than to bring a live mouse into a sewing circle. A government department wishes for honest and able men; but the kind of ability it desires is the ability which will run in harness, an unoriginative industry, a mind plastic to the will of its superiors. The Colonial Office had no fancy for a turbulent, great-hearted, idealistic Howe, with views on Imperial consolidation, who avowedly wanted office as a means of influencing the British public, and if possible of entrance into the Imperial parliament. Colonial secretaries were little likely to choose as their assistant the man who had taught Lord John Russell his business, who had first forced Lord Grey to do violence to his cherished convictions, and later on had accused his Lordship of lack of courtesy, if not of honesty.

Moreover, the Colonial Office of the day was, as a rule, in the control of men who thought the Empire was big enough, if not too big. Honestly doing their duty in the station to which it had pleased God to call them, they yet, most of them, had a half-formed thought that the natural end for a colony was independence, and had no mind for Imperial consolidation.

Howe knew all this; he knew that to them he was only a colonial, and Nova Scotia only a detail; he knew that all his services counted for less in their eyes than did the claims of some 'sumph' whose father or uncle could influence a vote on a division. He knew that for the English statesman of the day, as for the Nova Scotian, charity began at home. Unfortunately, his knowledge did not turn him to the idea of building up a great Canada wherein a man could find satisfaction for his utmost ambition; his larger loyalty had ever been to England. It was eastwards and not westwards that the Nova Scotian of his day turned for a career.

A man in this mood, with no job big enough to occupy his mind, full of an almost open contempt for his Nova Scotian colleagues, was a very doubtful asset to a government. Yet he could not be dispensed with, for in or out of the provincial Executive he was indisputably the foremost figure in the province. To him the Cabinet turned so often for advice in hours of crisis that he became known as the 'government cooper'; and a government which is known to depend upon a power behind the scenes is invariably weakened.

In 1854 the Crimean War with Russia had broken out. Great Britain had enjoyed profound peace since Waterloo, and the mechanism of the War Office was rusty and inadequate. She soon became hard pressed for troops, and under the Foreign Enlistment Act Howe was sent, in 1855, by the lieutenant-governor of Nova Scotia to the United States with the object of getting men to Halifax, there to be sworn in. It was a delicate and unthankful task. Men did not come forward with enthusiasm, and Howe was driven to employ doubtful methods and doubtful agents. The sympathy of the United States was with Russia, a sympathy especially shown by the thousands of Roman Catholic Irish who had arrived in the past ten years. As a result of the attempted enlistments, Mr Crampton, the British ambassador, was given his passports by the American government; in New York Howe was mobbed, and compelled to escape from his hotel through a window. Meanwhile, the Irish in Nova Scotia had been roused against him. He returned from a mission on which he had hoped to win Imperial reputation under a cloud of failure, out of pocket, and with the Catholic vote, for the past twenty years his sheet-anchor, alienated.

Other misfortunes followed. Of late there had been rising into prominence in the Conservative ranks a country doctor, Charles Tupper by name. In 1852 he had demanded to be heard at one of Howe's meetings. 'Let us hear the little doctor by all means,' said Howe, with contemptuous generosity. 'I would not be any more affected by anything he might say than by the mewing of yonder kitten.' So vigorous was Tupper's speech that a bystander muttered that 'it was possible Joe would find the little doctor a cat that would scratch his eyes out.' In 1855 the prophecy was fulfilled. In his own county of Cumberland Howe was defeated by Tupper, and throughout the province the Conservatives obtained a decisive majority. In the next year Howe was elected for the county of Hants, but before he took his seat events occurred of which he took a short-sighted advantage.

The Irish Catholics of the province, whose numbers were now largely increased by the prospect of work on the railways, were for the most part hostile to the Protestant population. In face of their undoubted provocations, an equally narrow and irrational Protestant feeling was aroused. Late in 1856 this latent bitterness was roused to fury by a brutal attack by some Irish Catholics upon their fellow-labourers at Gourley's Shanty, along the line of railway construction. So savage was the fighting that the military were called out to restore order, which was not done without bloodshed. Howe saw his chance of revenge for the unjust treatment he had received at the hands of the Irish the year before—a chance of forming an almost solid Protestant party, on the back of which he might ride to power again. Beginning with justified condemnation of lawlessness and fanaticism, the lust of conflict and the delirium of the orator soon swept him into a campaign of attack, and led him to ridicule some of the most sacred tenets of Catholicism.

It is a sad spectacle. Howe had noble ideas of religious freedom. In his early struggle against the Oligarchy, when accused of hostility to the Church of England, he had said, and said with deep sincerity: 'I wish to see Nova Scotians one happy family worshipping one God, it may be in different modes at different altars, yet feeling that their religious belief makes no distinction in their civil privileges, but that the government and the law are as universal as the atmosphere, pressing upon yet invigorating all alike.' A few years later, in his struggle for one undenominational college, he had taken the same generous stand. In 1849, at a time of great bitterness, he had supported, before the English of Quebec, the rights of the French-Canadian Catholics. 'How long will you be making converts of the compact mass of eight hundred thousand French Canadians, who must by and by multiply to millions, and who will adhere all the more closely to their customs and their faith, if their attachment to them be made the pretext for persecution? In the sunshine, the Frenchman may cast aside his grey capote; but, depend upon it, when the storm blows, he will clasp it more closely to his frame. You ask me what is to be done with these recusants? Just what is done now in Nova Scotia on a small scale, and by republican America on a large one: know no distinctions of origin, of race, of creed. Treat all men alike.'

Yet now we find the same Howe shrilling forth the very blasts of persecution which he had denounced. Provocation he had—bitter, violent provocation. But he had yielded place unto wrath; his egoism, his worship of success, were getting the better of his nobler side.

He had his reward. In 1860 his party was victorious at the general election. For the next three years he was in office, outwardly the same cheery Joe as ever, inwardly distracted, rebellious, pining for a wider field. But in 1863 Tupper and the Conservatives swept the province with the cry of retrenchment. In a house of fifty-four Howe had but fourteen followers. For the moment he was glad to be quit of office. 'If ever I can be of use to Nova Scotia, let me know,' were his words to Dr Tupper as he handed over the keys of the provincial secretary's office. Later in the year he accepted from the Imperial government the important post of Fishery Commissioner. He was sixty years of age, and his part on the political stage seemed to have been played. But to the drama of his life a stirring last act and a peaceful epilogue were to be added.

Ever since the American colonies had torn away, the plan of a union, legislative or federal, of the remainder of British North America had been mooted, and nowhere with greater favour than in Nova Scotia. Geographical difficulties long made it an impossibility, but the steam-engine gave man the triumph over geography, and by 1860 an intercolonial railway, though not built, was evidently buildable. In 1864 the exigencies of Canadian party politics forced federation to the front with startling suddenness. Weary of long jangling, resulting in a deadlock which two elections and four governments within three years had failed to break, the nobler spirits of both parties in Canada resolved to find a solution in a wider federation. In the same year Dr Tupper had brought about a conference at Charlottetown, which met in September to discuss the question of Maritime Union. To this Howe, though a political opponent, had been invited, but pressure of work had prevented his attendance. Delegates from Canada persuaded the conference to take a wider sweep. Howe would now have liked to be present, but the season was getting late, and when he asked for a boat on the pretext of doing some inspection along the Island shore, the admiral on the station refused to furnish it. 'If I had had any idea of why he really wanted that ship, he could have had my whole squadron,' said the rueful admiral in after years.

After some preliminary talk, the members of the conference adjourned to Quebec, and there gradually wrought out the resolutions which are at the basis of the British North America Act. They then returned to their homes, to endeavour to secure the adoption of these resolutions by the legislatures and people of their several provinces.

In Nova Scotia rumours of dissatisfaction were soon heard. The merchant aristocracy of Halifax at once saw that free trade between the provinces, an essential part of the projected plan, would destroy their monopoly of the provincial market. They were wealthy and influential, and an opposition soon was formed, including members of both political parties. Their prospects of success hinged largely on the attitude of Howe.

At first it seemed as though for Joe Howe there could be but one side. It was taken for granted that he, who had spoken so many eloquent words, all pointing to the magnificent future of British North America, all tending to inspire its youth with love of country as something far higher than mere provincialism, would now be among the advocates of federation, and the wise and loving critic of the scheme to be submitted to the legislatures. Though his ideal had ever looked beyond to a wider Imperial federation, he had at his best always regarded Canadian federation as a necessary preparation for it. In the troublous times of 1849, when the Montreal merchants shouted for Annexation, he had urged Confederation as a nobler remedy. It had been the incentive to his work for the inter-colonial railway. In 1861 he had moved in the legislature a resolution in its favour. As late as August 1864, on the visit to Halifax of some Canadian delegates, he had been convivially eloquent in favour of union. While all this in no way committed him to the details of the Quebec plan, it went far to binding him to its principle. Yet it soon began to be rumoured that he was talking against it, and in January 1865 a series of letters on 'The Botheration Scheme' appeared in the *Morning Chronicle*, in which none could fail to recognize the hand of the veteran.

What were his objections to the plan? He sets them out in a letter to Lord John Russell in January 1865.

1. The Maritime Provinces, and especially his beloved Nova Scotia, are being swamped. A little later he wrote to another friend: 'I have no invincible objection to become an unionist provided any one will show me a scheme which does not sacrifice the interests of the Maritime Provinces.'

2. They will be swamped by Canadians, a poor lot of people, a little eccentric at all times, and at the worst given to rebellion—led by political tricksters of the type of his old enemy Hincks.

3. A federation is cumbrous, and inferior to a legislative union, such as that of the British Isles.

4. It will involve a raising of the low tariff of Nova Scotia, and ultimately protection.

To these arguments he afterwards added that a union of such widely scattered provinces was geographically difficult, and that it would arouse the suspicion and hostility of the United States.

These reasons, feeble enough at best, were at least political; unfortunately he had other reasons, deeper and more personal.

There can be no doubt that if he had gone to Charlottetown and Quebec, as one of the delegates, he would have thrown himself heartily into the project, and left his mark on the proposed constitution. It galled him that the Quebec scheme had been completed to the minutest detail, and published to the world, without any assistance from himself. He soon found that the people of the Maritime Provinces generally were averse to the scheme, and that many were already arrayed in downright opposition to it. What was he to do? He paused for a little. Two courses were open, one noble, one less noble. Not only in youth has Hercules' Choice to be made. Stern principle called on him to take one course, a hundred pleasant voices called on the other side. Was he to be the lieutenant of Dr Tupper, the man who had taken the popular breeze out of his sails, who had politically annihilated him for a time, with whom, too, his contest had been mainly personal, for no great political question had been involved between them; or was he to put himself at the head of old friends and old foes, regain his proper place, and steer the ship in his own fashion? In the circumstances, only a hero could have done his duty. There are few heroes in the world, and it is doubtful if modern statecraft conduces to make men heroic. And Howe was an egoist. Friends and colleagues had known his weakness before, but had scarce ventured to speak of it in public. In his cabinets he had suffered no rival. To those who submitted he was sweet as summer. He would give everything to or for them, keeping nothing for himself. They might have the pelf if he had the power. Proposals that did not emanate from himself got scant justice in council or caucus. This egoism, which long feeding on popular applause had developed into a vanity almost incomprehensible in one so strong, was not known to the outside world. But now, in his hour of trial, his sin had found him out. The real reason of his opposition was given in his savage words to a friend: 'I will not play second fiddle to that d—d Tupper.'

But the egoist was also 'a bonny fighter.' He flung himself into the fray as wild with excitement as any soldier on a stricken field. With every artifice of the orator he wrought the people of Nova Scotia to madness. It was poor stuff, most of it; coarse jokes, recrimination, crowd-catching claptrap. Eighty cents per head of population was, according to the agreement, to be the subsidy from the federal to the provincial government. 'We are sold for the price of a sheep-skin,' was Howe's slogan on a hundred platforms. Dr Tupper had passed a measure, instituting compulsory primary education, based on direct local assessment. In his heart of hearts Howe knew that it was a noble measure, such as he himself had wished to introduce but dared not; yet he did not scruple to play upon the hatred of the farmer against direct taxation. Instead of rousing, as of old, their love of Nova Scotia till it included all British North America and widened ever outward till the whole Empire was within, he made of it a bitter, selfish thing, localism and provincialism incarnate. Yet as an orator he was supreme.

Darkened so, yet shone
Above them all the archangel.

When the ablest speakers on behalf of federation met him on the platform, they were swept away in the blast of his ridicule and his passion.

In the midst of it his nobler self shone out again. The Reciprocity Treaty between Canada and the United States, negotiated by Lord Elgin in 1854, had been denounced by the government of the United States. To discuss this action, a great convention of representatives of the Boards of Trade and other commercial bodies of the northern and western States met in Detroit in August 1865, and was visited by Canadian delegates, of whom Howe was one. On the 14th of August he spoke as the representative of the British North American provinces. The audience at first was hostile. Gradually the skill and fire of the orator warmed them. At the last these hundreds of hard-headed business men rose spontaneously to their feet, and, amid tumultuous cheering, by a unanimous standing vote passed a resolution recommending the renewal of the treaty. Seldom can orator have won a more signal triumph.

For a time his anti-federation campaign went merrily, and received an impetus from the defeat in 1865 of the pro-federation government of New Brunswick. But Howe reckoned without the unflinching will of Tupper, a political bull-dog with a touch of fox. Though the province was obviously against him, the Conservative leader had a majority in the legislature in his favour. That this majority had been elected on other issues, and that the proper constitutional course was to consult the people, mattered not to him. Here was a big thing to do, and he was not the man to be squeamish on a point of constitutional correctness. He held his majority together by the strong hand. In 1866 he succeeded in getting a resolution passed, authorizing the sending of 'delegates to arrange with the Imperial government a scheme of union which will effectively ensure just provisions for the rights and interests of the province.' The Quebec Resolutions were not mentioned, but it was to support the Quebec Resolutions that the delegates went.

Howe also visited London, and endeavoured to sidetrack the federation scheme by a revival of his old idea of an organic union of the Empire with colonial representation in the Imperial parliament. To the pamphlet in which he put forward his views Tupper published a smashing reply, which consisted solely of extracts from Howe's own previous speeches in favour of British North American union. Against Howe he set Howe, and seldom was an opponent more effectively demolished. Meanwhile conferences between the representatives of Canada, New Brunswick, and Nova Scotia, presided over by the British secretary of state for the Colonies, wrought out the British North America Act. In March 1867 it became law, and on the 1st of July 1867 it came into force.

JOSEPH HOWE.
From a photograph by Notman, taken about 1871

What was Nova Scotia to do? At the first election subsequent to federation, among the nineteen Nova Scotian delegates, Tupper alone of the Conservatives was elected. Eighteen others, with Howe at their head, went to Ottawa pledged to secure repeal. In the local house, of thirty-eight members two only supported federation. Howe had his majority; but what was he to do with it? Repeal could come only from England, and to England Howe went. One good argument he had, and one only, that Tupper had refused to consult the electorate on a question involving their whole constitutional status as a province; that, as he put it, they had been entrapped into a revolution. With the aid of this he won the support of the great English orator, John Bright, and had the matter brought up in the House of Commons. But Bright's motion for a committee of investigation was voted down by an overwhelming majority.

Meanwhile Tupper, with fine courage, had followed him to London, and had made his first call upon Howe himself. Howe was not at home, but Tupper left his card, and Howe returned the call. Over forty years later the veteran, now Sir Charles Tupper, told in his *Recollections* the story of their interview.

'I can't say that I am glad to see you,' said Howe, 'but we must make the best of it.'

'When you fail in the mission that brought you here,' said Tupper; 'when you find out the Imperial government and parliament are overwhelmingly against you—what then?'

Howe replied: 'I have eight hundred men in each county in Nova Scotia who will take an oath that they will never pay a cent of taxation to the Dominion, and I defy the government to enforce Confederation.'

'You have no power of taxation, Howe,' Tupper replied, 'and in a few years you will have every sensible man cursing you, as there will be no money for schools, roads, or bridges. I will not ask that troops be sent to Nova Scotia, but I shall recommend that if the people refuse to obey the law, that the federal subsidy be withheld.'

'Howe,' he continued, 'you have a majority at your back, but if you will enter the Cabinet and assist in carrying on the work of Confederation, you will find me as strong a supporter as I have been an opponent.'

'Two hours of free and frank discussion followed,' writes Tupper. That very night Tupper wrote to Sir John Macdonald that he thought Howe would join the Dominion Cabinet.

On his return to Nova Scotia, Howe found that the extreme repealers in the local legislature were talking secession and hinting at annexation to the United States. He could countenance neither. The son of the Loyalist was loyal at the last. The whole province was like tinder. A spark would have kindled a fire that would have ruined it, or thrown it back ten or twenty years. Howe trampled the spark under his feet.

Meanwhile, in Ottawa, an unrivalled political tactician was watching the situation. While the fever in Nova Scotia was at its height, Sir John Macdonald had refused to say a word. Now that the fever had run its course, now that the one able leader of the repeal cause realized the *impasse* into which he had brought his beloved province, Macdonald saw that it was the time for him 'from the nettle danger to pluck the flower safety.' He entered into negotiations with Howe, employing all his art and all his sagacity. Clearly he put the choice. Nova Scotia was in the Dominion, and the only way out led direct to Washington. Was not the only possible course for the greatest Nova Scotian to sink his personal feelings, and to join in giving to Nova Scotia her due part in a nation stretching from sea to sea and from the Arctic to the Great Lakes, puissant and loyal beneath the flag of Britain?

Against this conclusion Howe fought hard. It meant for him an act of inconsistency which he well knew his recent allies would stigmatize as apostasy. But the logic of the situation was too strong for him, and with noble self-sacrifice he faced it. In January 1869 he entered the Cabinet of Sir John Macdonald, and by so doing won for Nova Scotia the better financial terms which removed her most tangible grievance. By this time most of the leaders of the repeal party were ready for this step, even though their followers were not. Had Howe sunk his egoism and consulted them before he crossed the Rubicon, had there been no telegraph between Ottawa and Halifax, so that he could have come personally and have been the first to explain to them the improved financial terms which he had won, and the necessity of his entering the Cabinet as a pledge of his sincerity, they would probably have been satisfied. But the telegraph spoiled all, especially as there were men in the local legislature who were fretting against his leadership. They felt themselves to be in a false position, from which they could escape by making Howe the scapegoat. For ten days the only fact that was made to stand out before all eyes was that the leader of the anti-confederate and repeal party had taken office under Sir John Macdonald. The cry was raised, Howe has sold himself; Howe is a traitor. They condemned him unheard. When he returned to Halifax, old friends crossed the street to avoid speaking to him, and young friends, who once would have felt honoured by a word, walked as close before or behind him as possible that he might hear their insults. He was getting old; during his labours in 1866 in England bronchitis had fastened on him; and now the love and trust of the people—that which had been the breath of his nostrils—failed him utterly.

Having accepted Cabinet rank, he had to resign his seat in Hants county, and to appeal to his constituents for re-election. The result was the fiercest fight in the history of the province. Money was openly lavished by both sides. Howe fought well, but his health gave way, and for the first time in his life his buoyancy and courage deserted him. Finally, at a little village where he and a prominent opponent were to face each other, Howe broke down, and sent a friend to ask his antagonist to postpone the meeting.

'Why must it be postponed?' was the reply.

'Sir, to speak to-night would kill Mr Howe.'

'Damn him! that's what we want,' was the fierce reply, symbolic of the merciless spirit of the contest.

Howe dragged himself to the platform, too ill to stand. Eventually he gained his election, but his health was shattered, and he was never the old Joe Howe again.

Then came the end. In the Cabinet he was not a success. He represented a small province with few votes, and even so he shared the leadership with Tupper. To Sir John Macdonald, too intent on a few great ends to have any place for unprofitable sentiment, the weary Titan was of less account than half a dozen Quebec or Ontario members with less than one-tenth of his ability, but with twice the number of votes in their control. Howe chafed under Macdonald's drastic though kindly sway, and by impetuous outbreaks more than once got the government into trouble. Late in 1869 he was sent to the Red River Settlement, in the hope of smoothing out the difficulties there. He did no good, still further weakened his health, and on his return was involved in a bitter quarrel with one of his colleagues, the Hon. William M'Dougall.

In 1872 he shared with Tupper the triumph of carrying in favour of the Conservative party eighteen of the nineteen seats in Nova Scotia, and of finally silencing the cry of repeal. In May 1873 his failing health led to his being appointed lieutenant-governor of Nova Scotia. He died suddenly on the 1st of June 1873.

Here, with a few words, we close our sketch of this man, the greatest that Nova Scotia has produced. Judging him not by single acts, as no one ever should be judged, but by his life as a whole, he may be called a great man. His honesty of purpose and love of country, his creative faculty, width of view, and power of will combined, entitle him to be called a great statesman. He was more than a politician and more than an orator. He had qualities that made men willing to follow him even when they did not see where they were going, or only saw that they were going in a direction different from their former course. Steering in the teeth of former professions, he bade them have patience, for he was tacking; and they believed him. True, they were swayed by his eloquence, and gladdened by his sympathy and his humour. The fascination of the orator thrilled them; but had they not believed that at bottom he was sincere, the charm would soon have ceased to work. As it was, they followed him as few parties have ever followed a leader. Men followed him against their own interests, against their own Church, against their own prejudices and convictions. Episcopalians fought by his side against the Church of England; Baptists fought with him against the demands of their denomination; Roman Catholics stood by him when he assailed the doctrines of their Church.

Though he was merciless in conflict, bitterness did not dwell in his heart. He was always willing to shake hands, in true English fashion, when the war was over. If friends expostulated about the generosity of his language or actions to political opponents, 'Oh! what's the use,' he would reply, 'he has got a pretty wife'; or, 'he is not such a bad fellow after all'; or, 'life is too short to keep that sort of thing up.' He was generous partly because he felt he could afford it, for he had boundless confidence in his own resources. This self-confidence gave him a hearty, cheery manner, no matter what straits he was in, that acted on his followers like wine.

The one thing lacking was that he had not wholly subordinated self to duty and to God. He was immersed in active engagements and all the cares of life from early years. He was capable of enjoying, and he did enjoy without stint, every sweet cup that was presented to his lips. He was conscious of great powers that never seemed to fail him, but enabled him to rise with the occasion ever higher and higher. Small wonder, then, that he cast himself as a strong swimmer into the boiling currents of life, little caring whither they bore him, because proudly confident that he could hold his own, or, at any rate, regain the shore whenever he liked.

A thorough intellectual training would have done much for him. The discipline of a university career enables even a young man to know somewhat of his own strength and weakness, especially somewhat of his own awful ignorance; and self-knowledge leads to self-control. Circumstances put this beyond his reach; but something more excellent than even a college was within his reach, had he only been wise enough to understand and possess it as his own. In his father he had a pattern of things in the heavens; a life in which law and freedom meant the same thing; in which the harmony between his own will and the will of God gave unity, harmony, and nobleness to life and life's work. The teaching of the old Loyalist's life was the eternal teaching of the stars:

Like as a star
That maketh not haste,
That taketh not rest,
Let each be fulfilling
His God-given hest.

But the veins of the son were full of blood and his bones moistened with marrow. Passion spoke in his soul, and he heard and loved the sweet voices of nature, and of men and women. Not that the whispers of heaven were unheard. No; nor were they disregarded; but they were not absolutely and implicitly obeyed. And so, like the vast crowd, all through life he was partly the creature of impulse and partly the servant of principle. Often it would have been difficult for himself to say which was uppermost in him. Had he attained to unity and harmony of nature, he could have been a poet, or a statesman of the old heroic type. But he did not attain, for he did not seek with the whole heart. And he puzzled others, because he had never read the riddle of himself.

All Nova Scotians are glad that he spent his last days in Government House. It was an honour he himself felt to be his due—a light, though it were but the light of a wintry sun, that fell on his declining days. Many old friends flocked to see him; and the meetings were sometimes very touching. An old follower, one who had never failed him, came to pay his tribute of glad homage. His chief had reached a haven of rest and the height of his ambition. When the door was opened, the governor was at the other end of the room. He turned, and the two recognized each other. Not a word was spoken. The rugged face of the liegeman was tremulous. He looked round; yes, it was actually old Government House, and his chief was in possession. After all the storms and disappointments, it had actually come to this. The two men drew near, and as hand touched hand the two heads bowed together, and without a word they embraced as two children would. Are there many such little wells of poetry in the arid wilderness of political life?

On the day of his arrival in Halifax a true and tried relative called. 'Well, Joseph, what would your old father have thought of this?' 'Yes,' was the answer, 'it would have pleased the old man. I have had a long fight for it, and have stormed the castle at last. But now that I have it, what does it all amount to? I shall be here but a few days; and instead of playing governor, I feel like saying with Wolsey, to the Abbot of Leicester:

An old man, broken with the storms of State,
Is come to lay his weary bones among ye;
Give him a little earth for charity.'

That was almost all that was given him. The only levee he held in Government House was after his death, when he lay in state, and thousands crowded round to take a long last look at their old idol.

On the morning after Howe's death a wealthy Halifax merchant, one who had been a devoted friend of his, saw as he was entering his place of business a farmer or drover, one well known for 'homespun without, and a warm heart within,' sitting on a box outside near the door, his head leaning on his hand, his foot monotonously swinging to and fro, looking as if he had sat there for hours and had no intention of getting up in a hurry. 'Well, Stephen, what's the matter?' 'Oh, nauthin',' was the dull response. 'Is it Howe?' was the next question, in a softer tone. The sound of the name unsealed the fountain. 'Yes, it's Howe.' The words came with a gulp, and then followed tears, dropping on the pavement large and fast. He did not weep alone. In many a hamlet, in many a fishing village, in many a nook and corner of Nova Scotia, as the news went over the land, Joseph Howe had the same tribute of tears.

Vex not his ghost; O let him pass! he hates him
That would upon the rack of this rough world
Stretch him out longer.

He sleeps in Camphill Cemetery, not far from the pines and salt sea water of his boyhood, a column of Nova Scotian granite marking his resting-place; and his memory abides in the hearts of thousands of his countrymen.

BIBLIOGRAPHICAL NOTE

Besides the two noble volumes, *Speeches and Public Letters of Joseph Howe*, edited by Joseph Andrew Chisholm, K. C. (Halifax, 1909), the reader should consult the biography of Howe by Mr Justice Longley in the 'Makers of Canada' series, and the account of Nova Scotian history by Professor Archibald MacMechan in *Canada and its Provinces*, vol. xiii. See also *Recollections of Sixty Years in Canada* by Sir Charles Tupper (London, 1914); and, in this Series, *The Winning of Popular Government* and *The Railway Builders*. For an intimate study of life in Nova Scotia there are no books equal to the works of Thomas Chandler Haliburton.

Milton Keynes UK
Ingram Content Group UK Ltd.
UKHW030743071024
449371UK00006B/605